*The Wells County Historical Society
would like to thank Ossian State Bank for their
generous financial support of this book.*

The history of banking in Ossian begins with the Farmers State Bank being chartered November 1, 1912. Shortly after beginning business, the Farmers State Bank purchased the Bank of Ossian, which had been in operation since 1902. On November 29, 1912, the banks were consolidated.

In accordance with the law at that time, banking corporations were required to be rechartered each twenty years, and on October 19, 1932, a new charter was issued to Ossian State Bank. All the assets and liabilities of the former bank were assumed by the newly chartered bank and it opened for business under the new name on October 24, 1932.

Following the bank holiday declared by the president in March 1933 and the revising of many banking laws and regulations, Ossian State Bank became a member of the FDIC with deposits insured up to $5,000. This law has been amended to give a maximum of $100,000 insurance to our depositors.

In 1948, the bank instituted a remodeling program by installing modern fixtures, lighting, acoustical ceiling, tile flooring, and an air conditioning unit. The constant growth and the increasing population of the Ossian area brought realization to the Ossian State Bank directors and officers that expansion would be necessary. By 1970, the bank was actively exploring expansion plans and after much thought, it appeared that the bank could best serve the community by staying in the downtown area. Adjacent properties were acquired and a new facility opened in September 1977. With continued growth in and around the Ossian community, the bank launched a significant expansion of their office in 1995. This doubled the bank's facilities to allow it to better serve the needs of a growing area. Sensing opportunities in the Bluffton market, Ossian State Bank established its first branch location in October 1998. Ossian State Bank continues as the only Wells County-based independent, community financial institution. With assets in excess of $75,000,000, Ossian State Bank is focused on serving the Northern Wells community with a glance towards the past and an eye on the future.

Ossian Branch

Bluffton Branch

Wells County
Towns and Townships

A Pictorial History

THE
DONNING COMPANY
PUBLISHERS

The Donning Company/Publishers
184 Business Park Drive, Suite 106
Virginia Beach, VA 23462

Steve Mull, General Manager
Ed Williams, Project Director
Debbie Williams, Project Research Coordinator
Dawn V. Kofroth, Assistant General Manager
Julia Kilmer-Buitrago, Associate Editor
John Harrell, Imaging Artist
Teri S. Arnold, Director of Marketing
L. J. Wiley, Graphic Designer

Library of Congress Cataloging-in-Publication Data:

A pictorial history of Wells County : towns and townships.
     p. cm.
  Includes bibliographical references and index.
  ISBN 1-57864-091-1 (hardcover : alk. paper)
   1. Wells County (Ind.)--History, Local. 2. Wells County (Ind.)--History,
Local--Pictorial works. 3. Cities and towns--Indiana--Wells County--History. 4. Cities
and towns--Indiana--Wells County--History--Pictorial works. I. Wells County Historical
Society.

  F532.W55 P53 1999
  977.2'72--dc21

                                                                99-049185

Printed in the United States of America

Front of Dust Jacket: Wells County Courthouse, 1929.
Back of Dust Jacket: Map of Wells County, 1876
Endsheet: Main Street in Ossian, Indiana, 1900.
Title Page: West Market Street in Bluffton, Indiana, early 1900.

CONTENTS

William Wells, namesake of Wells County, Indiana.
Born in 1770 in Kentucky. Abducted by Indians at the age of 14, later adopted by Little
Turtle, chief of the Miami at Fort Wayne. Assisted in negotiations between the Indians and
General Anthony Wayne. Served as Indian Agent there when the war of 1812 broke out.
Killed at the massacre at Fort Dearborn in 1815.

INTRODUCTION

Long before the first settler arrived in 1829 in what was to become Wells County, the area was claimed for the French by LaSalle in 1682. The entire area that drained into the Mississippi was named Louisiana in honor of the French King Louis XIV. The Peace of Paris in 1763 at the conclusion of the French and Indian War ceded this area to the English. England ceded the Northwest Territory to the United States by the Treaty of Paris in 1783.

During this period, a significant portion of Indiana was the home of the Miami Indians. They were land travelers, rather than canoemen, who lived in small villages at various suitable sites, which included camps along the Wabash River. It was reported by early settlers that there were small Indian camps within Wells County.

The Ordinance of 1787 established the organization and provision for the government of the Northwest Territory. In 1795, the Indians gave up their claim to much of Indiana at the Treaty of Greenville (Ohio).

The census of the Indiana Territory in 1815, a year before Indiana became the nineteenth state, listed 63,897 persons in Indiana, but no one at that time had settled in the area of Wells County. It was 1829 when Dr. Joseph Knox, a physician from New Jersey, arrived with his family and built a cabin across the river from the future site of the town of Murray.

Eventually patents were issued, each signed by the president in office at the time, for all of Wells County during the period between 1830 and 1853.

Travel was a hardship. Initially there were only trails to be followed through the hardwood forests; sometimes swampy wetlands and dense undergrowth impeded the traveler. For this reason, merchants opened general merchandise stores throughout the county to meet the needs of the settlers. Mills to grind the corn and wheat were erected along the streams where a race could supply water power. Soon other enterprises followed and a town was born. Eventually there would be fifty-two small towns and villages within the county, each providing essential goods and services for its area. Today, only nineteen or twenty can be recognized, although twenty-three were platted, with building lots staked out for businesses and residences.

Here is the story of those towns and townships, and the people who made them important in the history and heritage of Wells County.

The Stewart-Studabaker Victorian mansion, the home of the Wells County Historical Museum since 1974.

THE WELLS COUNTY HISTORICAL SOCIETY

The Wells County Historical Society was founded in 1935, initiated to plan the 1937 Centennial Celebration of Wells County. Its purpose then, as now, was to preserve the rich heritage of Wells County and its residents—past and present. The society has been fortunate to have many persons through the years interested in the society's mission. Donations of artifacts and important records have been made by both Wells County people and descendants from across the country. An internet web site has connected the society and our county with descendants and former residents who can keep in touch with their roots.

A museum for the collection, preservation, and display of Wells County related material was a goal first reached in 1953 when donated materials were displayed in a fourth-floor room at the courthouse. Growth of donated materials made it necessary to seek larger and more easily accessible museum quarters. In September 1967, the historic home of Dr. and Mrs. Clarence H. Mead was made available for a new museum location. Hard work by volunteers, who painted and restored the house, prepared the site for a dedication in May 1969. The museum was dedicated to "those who have preceded us, to whom we owe a great debt. We take great pride in their wisdom and foresight."

A dream for a permanent home for the society and museum became a reality with the society's purchase of the three-story French Second Empire style brick house built in 1882 by Alvin Stewart. Stewart had been the construction superintendent for the first railroad built through Wells County. A few years later it became the home of pioneer merchant John Studebaker, who had originally sold the land to Stewart. Many volunteers, some spending thousands of hours, restored the interior in Victorian style and refurbished and maintained the exterior. Over 10,000 catalogued items, all relative to Wells County are housed and displayed for public appreciation. The museum, on the National Register of Historic Places, has fourteen rooms, many decorated in late nineteenth and early twentieth century living style. A showpiece on the enclosed front porch is a 1904 curved-dash Oldsmobile donated by the family of the original owner.

Realizing a 100 year-old structure needs a complete and thorough restoration to weather another 100 years, concerned and interested persons have donated $250,000 for this work now in progress (1999). Climate control to preserve the priceless contents is included.

Besides the museum, many other activities, projects, and programs are regularly sponsored. Recently, in addition to this volume, were a *Wells County Cemetery Census,* a 1976 *History of Wells County,* a 1991 *Wells County Family History*, and the *Architectural Atlas of Wells County*, researched and compiled by Craig Leonard, architectural consultant, and a Wells County resident.

The Wells County Historical Society is proud of the many volunteers who are and have been making the past live on for the future. This volume is designed to add to that mission.

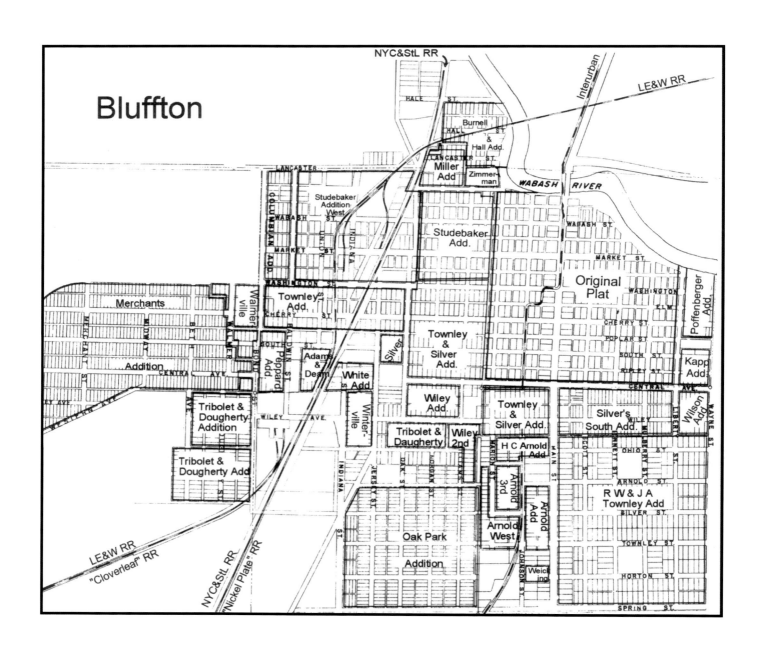

Bluffton

BLUFFTON

1

A BACKWOODS VILLAGE

The tiny village of Bluffton began its life under the most unpromising circumstances imaginable during the frigid winter of 1838. The only settlement in the entire county at the time was the little hamlet of Lancaster (later called Murray), and it consisted of only two or three log cabins and Jesse Gerhard's newly constructed flour mill on the Wabash. The rest was hardly more than a "howling wilderness," as an early observer noted.

The lands of the recently formed county were thickly forested and covered in many places with dark swamps and bogs. The few travelers who braved this well-nigh impenetrable tangle found the going difficult and discouraging. Most of them followed river beds whenever possible, as these were the only places where there was anything like a pathway through the forbidding woods. It was also along a river that one was most likely to encounter the lonely cabin of a trapper and his family, or per-haps a small clearing where a pioneer farmer was attempting to maintain a foothold in the wilderness. It followed, therefore, that the governmental center of the fledgling county should be situated on the Wabash River, which flowed diagonally across the center of the land area.

The location of the county seat had been chosen primarily because of inducements offered to the newly formed county government by two men who had recently purchased large land holdings in the area, Robert Bennett and Abraham Studabaker. The new settlement, called Bluffton by Bennett, was situated in an unpromising spot, although almost any place within the borders of the new county would have presented the same difficulties—a nearly impenetrable forest and murky swamps on all sides, clouds of malaria-carrying mosquitoes in summer, and flooding of the rivers and creeks in spring and early winter nearly every year.

Despite all its drawbacks, the little village of Bluffton began to attract settlers. Almon Case was the first to arrive, and after recovering from an attack of malaria he set up the town's first commercial enterprise, a log hut that he called a tavern. It was located on what is now the southeast corner of Main and Market Streets and was succeeded in 1840 by the Exchange Hotel, where a few years later the stagecoach for Fort Wayne could be boarded three times each week.

Soon after Case, young John Studabaker came with a wagon-load of trade goods, having been sent from Greenville by his father, Abraham Studabaker, to open a fur-trading post and grocery store on one of the town lots reserved to him. With money donated to the county's empty coffers by the Studabakers, work began at once on the two-story log and clapboard courthouse, which was erected in a clearing not far from the river bank, where the southwest corner of Wabash and Main is now located. A log jail was then built about three hundred feet to the south, where the present courthouse now stands.

Southeast corner of Main and Market. Almon Case's Exchange Hotel, shown here, was the stagecoach stop for many years.

Not far along the dirt path that was called Market Street, and separated from Studabaker's log-and-clapboard store by thick underbrush and trees, was Bowen Hale's little log cabin. Hale was the county clerk, and he, like Studabaker, dealt in furs and staple goods as well as whiskey. The two men cooperated in clearing the dense tangle of brush from the street, although the felling of large trees in the pathway had to wait for another day. For several

Northeast corner of Market and Marion. This is the oldest view of Bluffton. Note log and clapboard construction and wooden sidewalks.

Artist's rendering of the second courthouse and jail, constructed in the 1840s. They stood facing Main on site of the present courthouse.

years, in fact, large tree stumps could be found in the middle of most streets in the little town, forcing ox teams and farm wagons to detour around them as they made their laborious way from blacksmith shop to general store and back again to the tin smith's or the flour mill at the foot of Main.

By 1840 Bluffton had grown to a population of 225, and more people were arriving every month. Conditions remained relatively primitive, however, and the backwoods character of the place was evident for many years more. Dense forest surrounded the village on all sides, wolves were a constant menace to livestock, and the few schools and churches in the vicinity were housed in unprepossessing log or frame structures.

Education and religion were topics of the greatest importance to most of the little town's residents, and simple schools and houses of worship were among the first permanent institutions to be established. Starting with the Reverend George Bowers' first sermon on the banks of the river in 1838 and the Reverend Asa Cohoe's primitive log schoolhouse on the east side of the village in 1839, pioneer settlers began the long and arduous task of bringing civilization to the backwoods.

The log courthouse was destroyed by fire in 1844 and was replaced by a larger and more imposing brick structure the next year, complete with Doric columns and cupola in the Greek Revival style, but little else in the village showed much in the way of refinement or even permanence. Until 1869, the year the railroad connection to Fort Wayne was completed, dust-and-mud streets predominated, and according to a resident at the time "private houses and fences showed evidences of a general dilapidation and decay," while all along the line of shops and stores "battered and weather-beaten signs were creaking in the wind before pointless, rickety business houses." The little four-page weekly newspapers that sprang up from time to time here were intensely partisan but contained little more than idle gossip and harsh political invective.

PROGRESS AND PROSPERITY

All that began to change with the success of John Studabaker's railroad project in the late 1860s. A plank road, another of John Studabaker's proposals, had been laid between Fort Wayne and Bluffton starting in 1851, the same year the town was incorporated. This stop-gap measure had enabled Bluffton's shopkeepers to enlarge their stocks of goods and, more importantly, had provided an improved means of getting Wells County's agricultural products and timber to Fort Wayne, which was fast becoming an important regional railroad center. But the plank road, which generally followed an old Indian trail, was expensive to maintain and unreliable in bad weather, and it was obvious to everyone that a rail connection was badly needed. The general industrial revitalization that took place all through the North following the Civil War finally enabled Studabaker and his partners to push the rail line through to completion, and from that point forward the little town of Bluffton began to flourish.

The war itself had proven to be a serious issue within the county. While the northern townships were generally Republican in their sympathies, Bluffton, the county seat, contained a large number of so-called Copperhead Democrats, who had opposed the war against the Confederacy. One of the Copperhead leaders had been Theodore Horton, who was later to become an important local manufacturer. Bluffton had witnessed anti-government protests and even the hanging of President Lincoln in effigy during the darkest days of the conflict, but the presence of the railroad by the end of the decade helped to bring Wells County together once again. In every age, prosperity is a great unifier.

While the most rapid industrial progress in the nation during this period had to do with iron, steel, and the steam engine, there was a huge market for wood products as well. Now that Bluffton was connected to the great market centers of the nation through its railroad links to Fort Wayne and Cincinnati, the timber, staves, furniture, wooden wash tubs, axe handles, and finished lumber turned out by Bluffton's mills and factories brought prosperity to the town and an influx of new workers to add to the growing population.

Bluffton had achieved a population of 1,132 by 1870. A number of new stores and factories opened for business soon after the advent of the daily trains that shuttled back and forth between Bluffton and Fort Wayne. By the time of the Centennial in '76, several handsome new brick buildings had been erected in the business district, including the Curry Opera House on North Main Street and the so-called Centennial Block just west of the courthouse on Market. A new cemetery, Fairview, was opened in 1874 on the Division Road, just a short distance from the Main Street bridge.

During the 1870s and 1880s most of the old log and clapboard structures were pulled down and replaced by frame or brick houses built in the Italianate style. Much of the surrounding forest had now been cleared, and aggressive ditching had begun to conquer the swamps in which the pestilential hordes of mosquitoes bred each summer. Cattle and pigs continued to roam the muddy streets at will, and every house and public building had a privy "out back," but drinking water, after 1886, was cleaner and safer because of the town's up-to-date new

John Studabaker's first grain elevator, located near the bridge on N. Main.

Loungers and idlers found the wooden sidewalk in front of the Central Hotel a fine place to pass the time at the southwest corner of Market and Johnson.

John Studabaker moved this house from Murray to 313 W. Market in 1840. By 1902 it was Bluffton's oldest surviving house.

waterworks, built that year on East Washington Street.

Another sure sign of progress was the founding, in 1881, of Bluffton High School by Professor P. A. Allen. Although opposed by conservatives who felt that public schooling beyond grade school was a waste of money, Allen persisted and organized a classical curriculum that was soon the envy of neighboring communities. In 1890 an imposing new high school building was constructed on the southeast corner of Washington and Oak streets, next to the ten-room Central School, and this was soon followed by a new Columbian School in the western part of town. Washington Park School served the needs of the eastern side.

By the end of the 1880s, Bluffton had grown to a population of about 4,000, had spacious brick school buildings that housed over 900 pupils, and boasted a fire-alarm telegraph system, 104 street lamps, three newspapers, and seven miles of macadamized streets, among a host of other improvements. In addition, imposing new houses were being built to show off the new-found affluence of Bluffton's merchants and manufacturers. Notable among these were the Stewart-Studabaker House in the French Second Empire style, the McFarren House in the Queen Anne style, and the Henry Walmer House and the E. H. Montgomery House in the Italianate style.

A new iron bridge was built across the Wabash at the foot of Main Street in 1887, and the next year the cornerstone was laid for the present courthouse on the site of the old building, which had outlived its usefulness. When the new Romanesque-style courthouse was completed in 1891, its 130-foot clock tower dominated the business section of the town, and the huge structure's ample dimensions and ornate, fanciful stone decorations were a source of pride to the whole county. Although often drowned out now by the sounds of diesel engines, heavy truck traffic, and swarms of automobiles, the stately, sonorous striking of the hours from the great tower has been a reassuring accompaniment to the rhythms of ordinary town life down through the years.

THE OIL BOOM

The discovery of a rich oil field in the southern tier of townships brought unprecedented prosperity to Bluffton in the 1890s and beyond. New wealth prompted extravagance and ostentation in some cases, but solid investment in the form of new businesses and factories was also a result of this sudden windfall. Some local firms, like the Nimmons Stave Factory and the Grimes Foundry, profited directly from contracts with drilling companies or refiners, but others, such as the Marcy Manufacturing Company, which was later called the Red Cross Manufacturing Company, benefited indirectly from the fact that capital was available here to finance construction of their new large buildings. Nearly the entire downtown commercial district was transformed during the period from 1890 to 1905, with large brick buildings displaying facades in the Queen Anne

The 100 block of W. Market, directly opposite the courthouse as it appeared before the present brick and stone buildings were erected.

The east-west narrow gauge railroad generated much excitement when it was first proposed in the 1870s.

Theodore Horton's washing machine factory was located on W. Cherry Street. Horton was a well-known "Copperhead" Democrat and a very vocal critic of Lincoln during the Civil War.

The third Wells County jail was built in 1880. It was located on the present site of the Wells County Public Library, southwest corner of Washington and Johnson.

Monster Sale of Buggies.

At Sheldon, Ind., August 12th, at 11 o'clock, a. m., 1881, by Taylor & Sons. Music by the cornet and string bands, a stand of Eatibles, Lemonade, Ice-cream, &c., during the day, a grand Ice-cream supper in the evening. All are invited.

A forerunner of today's popular car auctions.

and Neoclassical styles replacing the last vestiges of the backwoods era.

With the construction of the city's sewer system and the paving of its major streets, the stage was set for the appearance of a large number of ornate new private houses on West Market and South Main. These were equipped with central heating, grand staircases, indoor toilets, stained glass windows in dining rooms and entry halls, and elaborate mantelpieces, moldings, and chandeliers throughout. On streets like Central, Cherry, South, and Wiley, more modest houses were being built, generally, but the trend was unmistakably toward embellishments and conspicuous comforts. It was about this time that the citizens of Bluffton began referring to their town as "the Parlor City." This was due to the very pleasing appearance of the place, which people said was "as neat and clean as a parlor."

Fashionable clothing was equally on display. Local papers carried regular advertisements for ready-made finery for men, women, and children alike, and readers were assured that anything purchased locally was "the latest" and "the best." It had come to be a matter of great importance that Bluffton and its people should not be perceived as being out of step with the fashion centers of the east. Here as elsewhere, end-of-the-century clothes were characterized by excess, both in the wasteful amounts of fabrics employed and in the lavish use of decorative trim.

As the nineteenth century waned, the United States made its first foray into the heady realm of imperialism with a war against Spain in 1898. The "splendid little war," as its proponents liked to call it, attracted a number of eager young volunteers to the colors, and Bluffton furnished a company of infantry that was ultimately assigned to the Fourth Regiment. The men served generally without incident for a year and returned to Bluffton in April 1899, amid the cheers of the populace and adulatory speeches made by local politicians. But other, later volunteers didn't fare as well. Young Carl Buck, son of John Buck, owner of the Buck Handle Works, was killed by Philippine insurrectionists while serving with the army at Caveat in 1902. His father erected the first mausoleum at Elm Grove, the new cemetery, soon afterward to inter his son's remains.

With increased prosperity and expanded leisure time there was also a growing appetite for amusements of all kinds. Baseball was wildly popular, and rivalries with neighboring towns and villages were taken seriously. Chautauquas, for those with a cultural bent, were held both here and in nearly every neighboring town. Excursions by train to the lakes that lie several miles north of Bluffton were also common in summer, and families that could afford them built airy cottages there in which to enjoy cool lake breezes during the worst heat waves of July and August. Theater troupes regularly visited the so-called opera houses downtown, Curry's and Sixby's, and presented melodramas, minstrel shows, comedies, and, sometimes, musical fare such as the Gilbert and Sullivan operettas—"The Mikado" was a favorite for many years. Skating was popular with the young, both on the ice in winter and on special hardwood rinks that were set up under canvas during the summer months. Ice cream socials, huge family reunions, picnics at Boiling Springs (just a few miles up Lovers' Lane, near Murray), croquet, horseshoes, and bicycle races were the favorite entertainments of many, but fairs and circuses were probably the most popular pastimes of all.

Fairs were common enough, and nearly every little town around had some kind of harvest-time celebration, usually in connection with a race track, for horse racing was immensely popular with both rural and town dwellers. But gambling and petty crime were also customary ingredients of such fairs, and Bluffton wanted to avoid any hint of that in the new Street Fair that was being planned by the Retail Merchants' Association. Consequently, horse racing played no part in the festival that was inaugurated on September 28, 1898.

The unique features of this fair were that admission was free and that it was being held on the newly paved streets of the town, away from the usual mud and dust of the country fairgrounds. Big crowds attended, drawn by the promise of free acts, good food, a well-planned agricultural exhibition, and the usual merry-go-round and Ferris wheel, in addition to sideshows and strolling bands. "The Fair," as Bluffton people have referred to it ever since, has been an annual event for nearly every one of the hundred years since its inception at the end of the nineteenth century.

THE NEW CENTURY

The town of Bluffton entered the new century with a sense of pride in its accomplishments and a decided optimism concerning the future. Its population had reached five thousand, and it could boast that its products were being shipped all over the world. Washing machines, windmills, water pumps, oil-field equipment, gloves and mittens, folding chairs, lawn swings, and barrels, as well as overalls, handles for tools, and cigars were produced in local shops and factories. By 1905 there were indications that the oil field south of Bluffton was losing favor with the big producers, who were now turning their attention to Oklahoma and Texas as sources of the next big "strikes," but by now the robust local economy seemed to have developed a momentum of its own that no longer required infusions of oil money to keep it moving.

The A. J. King Piano Company of Chicago built a large piano factory on West Wiley Avenue in 1908 and thus established an industry that for many years

Racial prejudice in Bluffton was prevalent for many years, reinforced by odious caricatures such as this one from the Bluffton *Banner* in 1882.

The first Central School (on the left) was built in 1868. The first high school building, on the right, was completed in 1890. The high school was moved to a new location in 1924.

The Columbian School was built in 1893 and served the west side of town for sixty-eight years. It was replaced by a new Columbian School in 1961.

played an important part in Bluffton's economy. The King Company was bought out by the H. C. Bay Company a few years later and was expanded greatly in 1918, to become one of the largest builders of pianos in the world. A rival company was begun in 1923 by B. K. Settergren, who established his factory in the old W. B. Brown furniture concern at the corner of Bond and Lancaster Streets. Settergren later renamed his firm the Estey Piano Company. From 1923 to 1928 the two factories, Bay and Settergren, were both marketing pianos, but the Bay Company went into receivership in 1928 and Settergren remained as the sole builder of pianos in Bluffton. For over forty more years, his company turned out Estey grand pianos, baby grands, upright models, and a handsome small upright of only five octaves, termed by some a "boudoir piano" and rumored to be popular in South American bordellos.

Improved rail facilities included an interurban link to Fort Wayne and Indianapolis and an east-west line to Huntington and Celina, Ohio, in addition to the original Fort Wayne-Chicago connection. It would not be long before better roads and highways and the availability of inexpensive automobiles and trucks would diminish the importance of rail travel and rail freight, but for a brief time in the new century little Bluffton was linked to a nation-wide web of steel rails that made nearly every corner of the nation accessible to it. Travel for recreation was no longer the prerogative of the rich alone, and trips to Chicago or St. Louis or New York for ordinary folk often began at one of the local train stations or at the downtown interurban depot on Washington Street.

The lure of the automobile would not be denied, however. The new brick and asphalt streets of Bluffton and the three hundred miles of gravel roads in the surrounding county were an inducement to drive a "machine," as early cars were often called. Travel by horse and buggy was slow and cumbersome and full of annoyances, and after the first few noisy, awkward cars had made their appearance here it wasn't long before the automobile became a familiar sight on the thoroughfares of Bluffton.

The introduction of such an innovation wasn't without its difficulties, however. As more and more young people learned to drive, speeding became a problem on local streets. In those early days, fast drivers were called "scorchers," and the police chief solemnly warned them through the newspaper that their scorching would bring the full weight of law down upon them if they didn't mend their ways. Many older people were wary of the auto, and as late as 1908 Fairview Cemetery banned them from its grounds, on the basis that they were noisy, disruptive, and undignified.

In 1905 the handsome new Bluffton Public Library was opened on Washington Street. The philanthropist Andrew Carnegie donated the bulk of the funds necessary for its construction, but a significant portion was subscribed by local citizens as well. There had been a circulating library available to Bluffton's citizens since the 1850s, but until now the collection had not had a permanent home of its own. The library expanded its collection rapidly and was soon a potent force among the educational resources of the town.

Bluffton's schools were under the direction of a brilliant young superintendent, William Wirt, whose educational philosophy was embodied in a plan he called "the platoon system." Its main features were the operation of the schools on a year-round basis, an elective scheme that permitted students to move through all the grades as quickly as they could master the material, and the stipulation that all pupils, of whatever age, be required to spend part of each day doing manual work of some sort, primarily in handicrafts, carpentry, and gardening. From most accounts the plan worked well and made the learning experience pleasurable as well as intellectually stimulating, but there were some drawbacks. Ambitious and insatiably curious young people sometimes breezed through the curriculum at an alarming clip and were qualified for graduation from high school at the tender age of fifteen, which was deemed far too young for matriculation at a college. What to do with these prodigies for the next three years was the problem facing their perplexed families.

The platoon system collapsed in 1907, when Wirt left Bluffton to set up the new school system at Gary and took most of his best teachers with him. P. A. Allen was then prevailed upon to return to the superintendent's position, and the schools reverted to the familiar classical curriculum that he favored.

Mr. Allen, as he was known to everyone, remained as superintendent until 1926 and continued to occupy an office in the Central School building as superintendent emeritus until shortly before his death in 1942. Many who were elementary-school students during the late 1920s and 1930s remember with affection the portly, white-haired old gentleman who sometimes shuffled quietly into the classroom and slowly made his way down each aisle, bestowing subdued compliments on all and occasionally giving a gentle pat of benediction to the head of some earnest little scholar.

The so-called "twin bridges" at N. Main as they appeared in the early 1900s. The bridge on the left was used for the interurban electric railroad. Studabaker's Grove is seen at the far left.

Wells County's third courthouse, located on the site of second one, was completed in 1891.

TRANSITION AND TURMOIL

The twenty years between 1915 and 1935 witnessed significant social changes in the little city. The memorable flood of the Wabash in the spring of 1913 had caused great inconvenience for all and, for a few, great hardship, but for the majority of Bluffton's population it was only an occasion for snapping a few pictures of the high water with the family Kodak. Far more serious was the effect of the European war, which broke out in the summer of 1914. America attempted to remain neutral, and frequent reminders could be found in local newspapers that the country was made up of people whose forebears had come from a wide variety of nations, including the chief belligerents. But following the sinking of the *Lusitania* in May 1915, anti-German feeling increased everywhere, and by the time of America's entry into the war in 1917 a virulent form of prejudice was being experienced by local families whose names were noticeably German in origin. Businesses run by "Germans" were boycotted by many, individuals were ostracized socially, and ludicrous stories were circulated about "spies" and "enemy agents" whose only crimes were a fondness for the Victrola records of Madame Schumann-Heink and a sentimental attachment to their distant relations back in Bavaria or Hanover. In some cases, young men with German names experienced humiliating physical violence at the hands of over-zealous "patriots," and this led to feuds that persisted for many years after the war.

As for the war itself, brief as America's involvement was in the conflict, both volunteers and draftees alike experienced the terrors of battle. Some gave their lives, and others returned permanently scarred by poison gas or shell-shock. Nearly all who came back were altered by the experience. Some were convinced that America must never again be lured into a European war, while for others their military adventures had led them to a broader and more liberal outlook on life.

The relaxed attitudes of wartime led to noticeable changes in ordinary existence in Bluffton. Work was increasingly more mechanized on surrounding farms and in the factories in town. Trucks were now widely used for freight-hauling, and automobiles and motorcycles were common sights on the streets. More and more women were driving cars, which were now being produced more cheaply than ever before, and fashions mirrored the new ease and freedom that women felt in the post-war era. Women's clothing was less restrictive, skirts were shorter in length, and the torturous corset was fast being relegated to the dust-bin. The Nineteenth Amendment to the Constitution finally gave women the vote in 1920, and along with political freedom came increasing social liberation as well.

The movies, which had developed and grown roughly in parallel with the new century, increasingly influenced ordinary behavior. There were three movie theaters in town at this time, the Grand on Washington Street, the Star in the Arnold Block on Main, and the Gaiety on East Market. The silent films they showed in the late teens and twenties not only validated the style changes that were evident everywhere, but also encouraged more freedom in language, social behavior, and sexual matters. Frankness and even coarseness were becoming more widespread, which didn't surprise many of the older generation, who had been decrying all this unwelcome change ever since the introduction of ragtime music back around the turn of the century.

Another constitutional amendment that had far-reaching effects locally was the Eighteenth, which prohibited the sale of alcoholic beverages nationwide and led to law-breaking on an unprecedented scale among the general population, including large numbers of people in Bluffton. Many felt that unreasonable restrictions had been imposed upon their private lives by a highly organized minority of prudes and hypocrites, and they had no intention of obeying such laws.

While "the Noble Experiment," as Prohibition's supporters liked to call it, didn't bring gangsters to the Parlor City, it was responsible for the presence here of a bootlegger or two, and it was said that a bottle of gin or whiskey could be procured in the lobby of the Bliss Hotel on most weekends, if one knew the right "traveler" to approach. It was also said in later times that there were always a couple of drugstores in town where one would buy "medicinal" alcohol without the fuss and bother of a duly signed doctor's prescription. Certainly, there was a large amount of homemade beer, called "home-brew," aging in crocks and bottles in the attics and cellars of various prominent citizens all during the fourteen years that the Eighteenth Amendment was in effect. A good home-brew recipe was treasured in the same way that the recipe for a delicious chocolate cake would have been jealously guarded by an outstanding cook. Elderberry wine, applejack, and cherry cordial were also popular alcoholic concoctions.

Telephones were common in houses by the twenties, although almost nobody had an extension phone, and many families were on party-lines. This meant they shared their service access with two or three other households and, presumably, only lifted their receivers when they heard their own pattern of rings issuing from the bell box—say, for example, two longs and a short. People were understandably much more guarded in those days about what they said over the telephone, as the temptation to eavesdrop was great, apparently.

Phonographs were still of the wind-up variety. A machine could be had quite reasonably from Ashbaucher's or Thoma's, and elaborate models in fine cabinets were available, too. Victor was still a name to be reckoned with where records were concerned, but Brunswick handled most of the popular dance recordings like the fox trot, as well as the leading jazz bands like Paul Whiteman and the newest craze among the young, the "crooners," Rudy Vallee and Bing Crosby.

The oil boom in the 1890s brought capital that helped to finance new businesses like the Bluffton Boot and Shoe Company.

Radio caught on quickly in Bluffton, due to the strong signals emanating from Fort Wayne, Detroit, and Chicago stations. The primitive technology of the crystal set had beguiled young readers of *Popular Mechanics* for years, and after commercial ventures like those of Atwater Kent and RCA were under way, it wasn't long before most middle-class homes in Bluffton boasted a set of some sort. Wells Electric and L. L. Bender's store, and later Fritz Electric, were among the places in town where you could buy a modest table-model or a big expensive floor-model. Radio cabinets were crafted of wood, primarily, and even the small ones were highly decorated with scrolls, miniature columns, and moldings. The big powerful sets were made to resemble richly detailed Renaissance bureaus or chests. Bluffton joined with the rest of America in listening to "Ma Perkins," "Little Orphan Annie," Lowell Thomas's news reports, "One Man's Family," "Amos and Andy," and of course during the Depression, President Roosevelt's "fireside chats."

The Depression had come as no great surprise to Bluffton and Wells County, inasmuch as a minor version of the economic upheaval had struck here in 1926, with the failure of most of the county's banks. Triggered by a drastic dip in agricultural prices in an atmosphere of general indebtedness, and further complicated by poor management of the assets of Bluffton's largest financial institution, the Studabaker Bank, the catastrophe wiped out hundreds of families' savings and severely hampered or destroyed small businesses countywide. When the national downturn began in 1929, local firms that had been barely hanging on began to weaken and go under, throwing many out of work. This in turn drastically affected shops and stores, which depended upon the purchases of workingmen and their families for their survival. Prices and wages plummeted, and a time of great hardship and anxiety set in for all. There was no unemployment insurance or social security in those days, nor were bank deposits insured. Unions were almost unheard of in the area.

Ashbaucher's store on W. Washington was filled with the fashionable decorative items popular in middle-class homes.

Some firms managed to survive by cutting back their work forces and their output, while still maintaining an aggressive sales staff that searched for every opportunity to transact business. The Red Cross Manufacturing Company, which was the town's largest employer, the Estey Piano Company, and the Patton-McCray Furniture Company were among those that remained open during the prolonged crisis, but there were close calls aplenty.

After the election of 1932 and the advent of President Roosevelt's so-called "New Deal" measures, there were noticeable changes in Bluffton. Government construction projects began to put laborers back to work, thus injecting money again into the local economy. New sidewalks were laid all over town, the sewage system was extended and upgraded with Federal funds and WPA labor, and a new bridge was built over the Wabash at Main Street. Schools benefited from a variety of programs, especially the new Park School, which was in large part financed with Federal money. Streets and roads were improved, and a new, state-of-the-art, three-lane highway was built between Bluffton and Fort Wayne along the route of State Road 1. A Civilian Conservation Corps camp was established east of town, near Vera Cruz, with the mission of building a state forest there. In addition to the recreational opportunities the park opened up for Bluffton's citizens, the camp also contracted for local goods and services, thus aiding the town's economic recovery.

During the worst days of the Depression, a few out-of-work drifters, called hoboes, rode into town nearly every day on freight cars of the Nickel-Plate railroad. They could often be seen in the alleys of

Fashions in the 1880s and 1890s were ornate and highly decorated. A woman's exaggeratedly narrow waist was achieved by wearing tight-laced corsets.

On W. Washington Street, a portion of the huge crowd that greeted the soldiers of Company E in April, 1899, when they returned from service in Cuba.

23

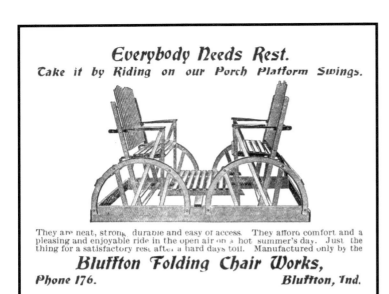

Another of the many wood products manufactured in Bluffton around the turn of the century.

Bluffton, shuffling from backdoor to backdoor to beg for a handout or perhaps a bit of work to do, in order to earn a little money with which to buy some food. These shabby, unkempt men were a powerful reminder that the economic woes of the nation were far from over, despite the many governmental plans that had been adopted to stimulate business activity and put them back into the workforce.

By the late 1930s, however, prospects were looking up again for most of Bluffton's citizens, although there were few adults who weren't aware that things had changed radically in their lifetimes. Those born at the turn of the century had grown up in a prosperous and optimistic Bluffton, a place of seemingly boundless opportunity, where diligence and hard work could earn one things like a big house, possessions of worth, and an honorable place in the local society; the Depression and its aftermath had changed those perceptions in large part, for it was abundantly clear that the larger world to which Bluffton was so inextricably bound was full of hazards and uncertainties. As if to underscore that somber truth, near the end of the decade two spectacular fires occurred that seemed to symbolize the harshness and riskiness of modern life.

Early in the morning of March 4, 1939, the people of Bluffton were awakened in their beds by the deep-throated, echoing blasts of the big steam-whistle at the waterworks, which was customarily blown at 6 o'clock each evening and was also used to alert volunteer firemen whenever there was a fire. Soon telephones were ringing all over town, as news spread about the raging fire at the Central School. Many families routed their sleepy children out of bed, hastily threw on their clothes, and made their way to West Washington Street to view the leaping flames and billowing smoke.

The full extent of the damage was apparent in the morning's light, after the fire had been extinguished. The high brick walls stood blackened against the sky and sunlight shone through the ruined roof and shattered windows. Here and there, in random piles at the doors and in the muddy yard were waterlogged heaps of textbooks, mildewed, smelling of smoke, and scorched; the remains of desks and pictures, and even the broken fragments of the so-called Grecian friezes (plaster casts of antiquities that had once graced the old high school), were troubling evidences of the fact that one of Bluffton's few cultural resources now stood in ruins.

Then in December, 1940, the Henry Arnold house on South Main Street was destroyed by fire. When it was first built in 1895, the house was the marvel of the day, a huge Queen Anne Style place with twenty-five rooms, innumerable porches and balconies, and a ballroom on its third floor. In the intervening years it had gradually ceased to be the most fashionable address in town, but it still represented the solid values of the old Bluffton.

Word of the fire spread rapidly, and soon a stupefied crowd stood on the wintry lawn watching in disbelief as the great gray house was consumed by flames, despite the efforts of the Bluffton Fire Department. While firemen battled the blaze on the upper floors, a steady stream of volunteers carried the drenched, bedraggled finery of the parlors to the sidewalk and to the house next door for safekeeping. It was apparent to everyone standing there under the great bare oaks of the Arnold estate that the old mansion was beyond salvaging, and that another like it would never be built again. They knew they were witnessing the end of a chapter in Bluffton's history.

Thus the conclusion of the 1940s, symbolically marked by conflagration and confusion, heralded a coming time of even greater upheaval and change—the wartime years of 1941 to 1945, and the resultant post-war period, which in many ways is with us still.

WAR AGAIN

Bluffton has never been invaded, bombed, occupied, or destroyed by artillery shells, of course, but America's wars have been felt deeply here and have certainly left their mark on the town in a number of very noticeable ways.

World War II evoked a jaunty, almost cheerful spirit in Bluffton at first. Its young men reported for induction without incident, and often eagerly, and acquitted themselves well wherever they were stationed. The prevailing spirit here at home seemed to be that there was a big, important job to be done, and we Americans were the people to do it. Everyone who was able threw himself willingly into war work. Few grumbled about rationing or shortages, although evidences of hoarding were abundant enough, too—toilet paper, sugar, and canned goods were favorite items to stockpile, and consequently there were backrooms and basement storerooms in private homes all over town that were off-limits to casual visitors.

The huge General Electric plant in Fort Wayne employed a large number of Bluffton workers, who made their way there and to other factories in the area each day by car-pool or bus. The interurban cars were no more after 1941, killed off by the irresistible spread of automobiles and the construction of better roadways. Both gasoline and rubber tires were severely rationed, but most people continued to drive whenever possible for recreation.

The lure of higher paying war-time jobs in Fort Wayne deprived local factories of many of their workers, and of course there were few young men entering the work force as new laborers. Many women for the first time took jobs, primarily to help out what everyone called "the war effort," but also to bring in extra

The Chautauqua grounds just north of the bridge. These lecture series were eagerly awaited each summer.

Case's Island, just west of Studabaker's Grove, was a favorite spot for picnicking and gathering wildflowers. The "old swimming hole" was nearby, too.

money for the family. This was to have far-reaching effects after the war was over and there was a dazzling array of new consumer goods available for purchase.

At the height of the war, in the summer of 1943, the Farnsworth Radio Corporation of Fort Wayne made plans to set up a factory in Bluffton for the manufacture of radio equipment for the army. The plant, which was located in the old Patton-McCray building on West Washington Street, eventually employed a work force of about 600, making it for a time the largest employer in the county. Bright hopes for the post-war presence in Bluffton of a large, permanent radio and television plant rapidly dwindled following the end of hostilities. Some Farnsworth-brand radios were produced here for the civilian market after 1945, but by 1950 the factory was ready to close its doors.

As the war lengthened and news filtered back about prisoners and casualties, things became much grimmer. Several young men were killed in action, and everyone could picture them as they had been only three or four years earlier, running down the hardwood in a close basketball game at the Community Building, or shuffling along in the autumn leaves, talking intently to pretty girls on the way home from school, vital and strong and full of hope for the future.

By the end of the war in the late summer of 1945, after the harrowing and costly last-ditch battles on both the German front and in the Pacific, and after the full horror of the concentration camps had been made plain through news accounts in the *News-Banner* and unbearably graphic newsreels at the Grand Theater, many longed to return to the peace and quiet of the pre-war world. But that was not fated to be—the war had unleashed economic and social forces that would soon begin to affect ordinary life everywhere, forces that would even have an impact on the familiar streets of Bluffton as it sat drowsing here by the muddy brown Wabash.

POSTWAR AND BEYOND

Over fifty years have passed since the end of World War II, but the new spirit that came to characterize Bluffton in the late 1940s and 1950s is with us still. The old Bluffton of pre-war days had been a place just small enough for everyone to be known by everyone else and appreciated for his or her own unique qualities. In the main, it was composed of families that had been here for generations. But after the war, in an effort to energize the local economy and avoid being left behind in the general rush toward prosperity, a vigorous push was made by the town's leaders to attract larger businesses and manufacturing enterprises to Bluffton. This campaign was successful, and new firms were soon settling here as old ones were expanding. All this activity not only drew upon the local workforce but also attracted workers, managers, and executives from far off communities. Many of these moved here permanently and thus increased the population and eventually brought changes in the social and political structure of the town.

Franklin Electric, Almco Steel Products Company, Sterling Casting, the James S. Jackson Company, and Bluffton Ready Mix were companies that were either founded in this period or expanded their operations significantly. The Red Cross Manufacturing Company, Estey Piano, and the Hoosier Condensery con-

Boiling Springs, up near Murray, was a pleasant spot for Sunday afternoon excursions.

For many years the intersection of W. Market and Marion was the site of the Street Fair's ornate merry-go-round. The ride was kept under canvas until the fair officially opened.

tinued to be important local employers, and the Caylor-Nickel Clinic and Hospital now joined the ranks of Bluffton's larger organizations. A variety of small manufacturing plants, machine shops, and food processors were also important parts of the economic mix. Among these were the A. W. Cotton Company, Houser Engineering Company, Bluffton Foods, the Bluffton Grocery Company, Steury Bottling, Pretzel Bitz, and local processing operations for the giant Libby and Heinz corporations.

The Corning Glass Works, which made glass tubes for the television industry, opened its big plant west of Bluffton early in 1965 and soon joined the ranks of the largest employers in the area. It, too, attracted workers and managers from far afield, and this had a definite impact on both the economic and social life of Bluffton. It came as a great shock to the town when, only eighteen years later, the entire plant was shut down by the Corning Corporation. World competition, in the form of cheaper Asian television tubes, had priced the Bluffton product entirely out of the market.

Labor unions were now an acceptable fact of economic life here, after some initial resistance on the part of the larger employers. Benevolent paternalism had worked well enough in the days of John Studabaker and B. K. Settergren, perhaps, but the modern distance between owners at the top and workers at the bottom was now so great as to be almost unbridgeable, and some equalizing mechanism was felt by many to be a necessity.

Perhaps one telling evidence of the widening gap between the well-off professional and managerial class and the great majority of

The King Piano Company was the first of three piano makers in Bluffton. It was located on W. Wiley Avenue. This view dates from 1909.

the citizens who worked for hourly wages was the rapid development after the war of the eastern section of the city known as Riverview. Prior to the war, in almost every neighborhood in town, bankers, physicians, and executives had lived next door to plumbers, electricians, small shopkeepers, and mechanics. Now, spending the money they had accumulated in the war years, many of these professional families built large, impressive houses overlooking the Wabash, or on the gently rolling terrain nearby. For the first time in its history, Bluffton was witnessing an overt foray into the realm of exclusivity by a sizable number of its most prominent citizens. The reaction was mixed. The invidious term "Snob Hill" was bandied about by those who were not amused, but generally in the acceptable American way, most of those left behind after this small exodus simply looked forward to the day when they too could afford to get a place over in the new suburb.

For everyone, regardless of their income, there was an almost unimaginable amount of leisure time available, compared to the unremitting toil expected of every man, woman, and child in Bluffton's pioneer days a century and a half before. The forty-hour week, so long a dream of radical reformers, was now a reality, and with it came both benefits and unexpectedly harmful side-effects that the entire nation had to contend with.

Paradoxically, with more leisure time available to all, church attendance dropped off. With more time to do it in, there were fewer recreations in town, too. Local movie theaters disappeared one by one—first the Roxie, then the

Grand, and finally the drive-in theater north of town. Local lodges and clubrooms witnessed a drop in their membership, and the dances they had sponsored and that had for many years been a major entertainment became less frequent, less elaborate, and less well-attended. During the late 1940s and through the 1950s teen hang-outs, usually drugstores with soda fountains like Hinkle's and Young's or confectioneries like Fryback's, had continued to be popular with the young. But the soda fountain, which had been a popular attraction in downtown Bluffton since the 1870s, eventually lost its charm, too, and disappeared for lack of patronage. The construction in recent years of the Wells Community Pool on the south side of town and the River Greenway along the Wabash has served to provide recreational opportunities to a wide variety of people, but the fact remains that most sit at home watching television in their spare time.

Television burst upon the local scene in 1948 with Gordon Hart's first public exhibition of the new technology. Within five years, sets were becoming common in town, even though a big, unwieldy antenna had to be erected on the highest peak of each roof if the signals from Fort Wayne were to be received clearly. The first sets were expensive, the screens were small, and the entertainment offered was often insipid and unimaginative, but television was still wildly popular. It kept many at home, and it was certainly responsible for the demise of the local movie theaters and other enteratinments. It was free and convenient, and although later it also became violent, salacious, and vicious, it continued to have nearly a hypnotic appeal for most of Bluffton's households. Many observers feel strongly that it has played a clear role in contributing to social and learning problems with the young.

Coupled with this development has been the proliferation of the automobile. The two-income family has necessitated two cars, and many indulgent parents have purchased cars for their teen-age children as well. Single parent families are all heavy users of the automobile, as work opportunities are seldom near home, and shopping and entertainment destinations are often far distant. The lack of parking space for a society that increasingly refuses to walk even a few short blocks has severely affected retail business in Bluffton's downtown area, too. Increasingly, Bluffton people shop on the north side of Fort Wayne, if they are not buying in the firms that have located north of the Main Street bridge along State Highway 1.

For a variety of reasons, several venerable old businesses that once seemed invulnerable to change have disappeared. The Red Cross Company by 1974 had lost seventy percent of its customary business and shortly thereafter closed its doors forever, after three-quarters of a century of successful operation as one of the town's chief employers. The Hoosier Condensery was eventually no more, nor were Estey or Patton-McCray or the Thoma firm, which had been in operation at the same location for 131 years. The Bliss Hotel fell under the wrecker's ball, as did the Grand Theater building, and the old Central School on West Washington.

Lincoln National Bank of Fort Wayne, owner of the Farmer and Merchants Bank, saw fit in the early 1990s to destroy half of the irreplaceable Arnold Block opposite the Courthouse for an eight-space parking lot. A large number of private homes in

Settergren's Piano Factory eventually came to be called the Estey Company. For many years it was one of the largest Bluffton employers.

The automobile and the horse co-existed for a decade or two, but the livery stables in town, like Seabold's on W. Washington, were doomed to extinction.

the vicinity of the Caylor-Nickel Clinic and Hospital have been purchased over the years by "The Clinic," as everyone calls it, and demolished to provide room for expansion and larger parking facilities. Other buildings and houses have come down in the name of progress and convenience, but generally what has really been meant was "parking." To anyone who is in the least bit historically-minded, the overall visual effect is one of random depredation.

What the future holds is, of course, impossible to know for certain. There are a few hopeful signs, fortunately. Most of the plastic and aluminum false-fronts that were for a brief time fashionable downtown have now been removed, and the elaborate nineteenth-century architecture is once again visible. Some of the big old houses in town have been rehabilitated, too, and even those that have been converted to businesses and offices or apartments are generally well-kept. Plans are being made to refurbish or replace sidewalks all over the city, and young trees are now regularly planted along the streets to replace those lost to disease or wind storms.

With continuing commitment to quality in all our endeavors—in our schools, in our business life, and in our relations with one another—we have reason to hope that Bluffton, which has endured much since its crude beginnings in the swamps and thickets of an unforgiving wilderness, will flourish in the new century that now lies before us.

–J. Foster

Many travelers, some headed for distant places like New York or even Europe, began their journeys at the Clover Leaf station.

A shipment of Delco generators arrives at the interurban freight warehouse. This location is now the alley that runs alongside the Parlor City Cafe.

Top photo: This interurban car has just come in from Fort Wayne and has stopped alongside the Grand Opera House on S. Johnson. Note the fire tower on the old City Building—now Republican Headquarters.

The old ice pond was located east of the present site of the Airplane Station. After the "ice plant" on W. Cherry began making ice artificially, this pond was used as the town's swimming pool.

The Famous ARGO $295

F. O. B. JACKSON, MICHIGAN

FOUR CYLINDERS, SHAFT DRIVE

Top, Winshield, Headlights and Generator Attached $29.00 Extra.

ARGO MOTOR COMPANY, Inc. Jackson, Mich.

R. L. and Ray O'Donnell, Agents Wells and Jay. Montpelier Route 11

Some still relied upon the horse for local excursions. This scene on Main in front of the Arnold Block dates from the summer of 1908.

The popularity of the auto was due in part to the availability of low-cost cars. Bluffton's newspapers carried ads like this frequently in the years following the First World War.

Setting out from Bluffton for a long journey by automobile was a real adventure. Roads were bad and "punctures" by the dozens could be expected.

More autos necessitated better street surfaces. Bluffton's streets were paved with asphalt or brick early in the century, leading to the town's nickname, "the Parlor City."

Part of the crew surfacing the streets downtown. The A. B. Cline house is in the background.

Motorcycles were another inexpensive form of early motorized transport.

The second Central School was built in 1910 on the site of the first one and served for many years as an elementary school, a high school, and a junior high. The play-yard was covered with gravel that was the cause of many a bloody knee or skinned elbow.

In town most people walked to the downtown stores. A few from the far end of S. Main or Villa North or W. Washington might have driven a buggy or a car to do their shopping.

Looking east from the courthouse at the turn of the century. Very few of these structures are still standing. The dirt road on the left is E. Market, while the one on the left is Walnut. The Community Building now occupies the area in the foreground.

The 1913 flood was the worst seen in many years, but most of the town was on high ground and was not affected. This picture was taken from the courthouse tower looking north.

These large airy porticoes were out-fitted with rockers and armchairs for lounging and observing the busy streets below. The Bliss Hotel, the Elks Club, and the Moose Lodge all had them.

One important outgrowth of the First World War was the construction of the Wells County Hospital in 1917. It was the forerunner of today's much larger Wells Community Hospital.

The Grand Theater, Bluffton's largest and most elaborate movie house, was located in the Grand Opera House building, southeast corner of Johnson and Washington.

West Market in 1921. The upstairs offices of the business section were as important as those on the ground floor. Doctors, dentists, lawyers, insurance agents, and the social rooms of various lodges were customarily located on the second floor.

Bliss Hotel, northeast corner of Main and Washington. Demolished 1961. Further down the street was the Arnold Block—half of which was torn down for a small parking lot.

One of the most popular spots in summer was the Psi Iota Xi pool, just south of town.

The Hoosier Condensery survived the Depression and was a major Bluffton employer for many years.

"Pete" Peters' Shell station was familiar to all who visited the Caylor-Nickel Clinic on S. Main. Pete started his working life driving a team for the Railway Express Agency, but like many others later made a good living from servicing cars and trucks.

The locally famous Airplane Station was built on the old Chautauqua grounds north of Bluffton by William Moser in 1931.

When the Arnold house burned in 1940,
it marked the end of an era. The big Queen Anne
Style house was located at 628 S. Main.

An inspiration to generations of young people was Charles Deam, Indiana's first State Forester and an unparalleled collector of native flora. His two books on the trees and shrubs of Indiana are still classics. Pictured here in his 1915 "weed wagon," in which he collected his botanical specimens.

These big Indiana Railroad cars had a difficult time competing against the automobile during the 1930s. The last one rolled through Bluffton in 1941.

Scenes from the long-departed past are poignant reminders of the swift passage of time. The Public Drug Store was on the northeast corner of Market and Johnson.

Members of this fetching group, daringly posed on the portico of the Bliss Hotel in the summer of 1908, have all departed now.

**All but two of these buildings have been demolished.
The structures at 121 and 125 N. Main are still standing.
Wolf Cycle Shop was in the Curry Building at 119 N. Main.**

Nash's Grocery was a familiar sight years ago to workers returning home from the Red Cross factory or the piano factory. All these landmarks are gone now.

Even the Dutch Mill, which since the 1940s had been a part of modern Bluffton, was subject to the whim of fate. The universally popular restaurant was completely destroyed by fire in the winter of 1998.

The great blizzard of 1978 was another reminder of the
power of nature. For a time it forced many of Bluffton's citizens
to revert to the primitive conditions of the 1840s.

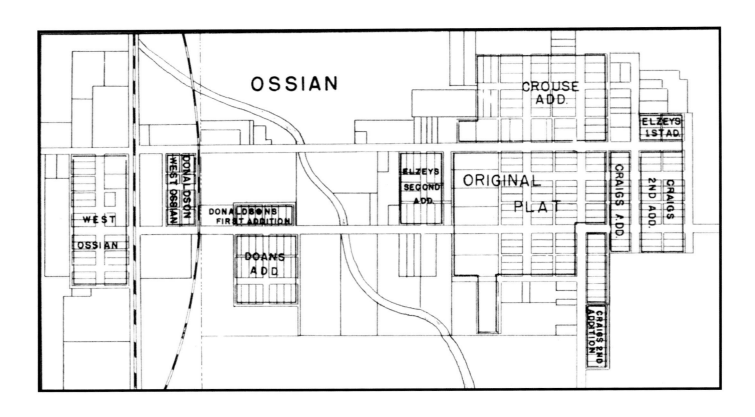

OSSIAN

WEST OSSIAN

DONALDSON WEST OSSIAN

DONALDSONS FIRST ADDITION

DOANS ADD

ELZEYS SECOND ADD.

CROUSE ADD.

ELZEYS 1ST AD.

ORIGINAL PLAT

CRAIGS A.DD.

CRAIGS 2ND A.DD.

CRAIGS

CRAIGS 2ND ADDITION

48

OSSIAN

2

BEE CREEK AND BEYOND

As has been noted many times by local historians, in its first years Wells County was a forbidding place of swamps, murky tangles of thick vegetation, and gloomy, almost impenetrable forests. Union and Jefferson townships, which depended upon the meandering vagaries of Eight Mile Creek, were even less hospitable than the rest of the county. Eight Mile Creek is a tributary of the Little River, which was itself infamous in pre-canal days for its frequent flooding and sluggish flow. Even today, almost monthly, the Wells County Drainage Board deals with difficulties surrounding Eight Mile Creek. An early account of the Ossian area by James Keefer conjured up a picture of "silent woods, dense and damp, distorted and disfigured by gnarled, swampy undergrowth."

A settlement was clearly needed somewhere along the northernmost part of the trail that connected Bluffton and Fort Wayne, a place with a store or two and perhaps a school, to serve as a market for local goods and a gathering place for the slowly growing farm community. According to Keefer, Levi Young, who arrived in the 1840s, was the first settler on the site of what later came to be called Ossian. John H. Glass built a small cabin, outfitted it with a rudimentary stock of supplies and commenced "keeping store" there shortly after the arrival of Levi Young. The cabin of Mr. Glass, which cost the grand sum of $16, was noted to be the best in the neighborhood, since it was a two-story structure boasting three windows and a good clapboard roof.

In 1845 Glass paid from one-half to three-quarters of a cent per pound for livestock, and since there were no scales available, he was allowed to guess at the weight. He had a good trade with Fort Wayne butchers and also dressed pork for John Studabaker, a Bluffton packer. After spending one summer in the wilderness, he concluded that it would improve his circumstances to have a permanent housekeeper, and so on December 24, 1846, he married Margaret Hatfield. This was the second marriage in Jefferson Township.

Other sources state that "into this wilderness of forest, water, swamp and ague, came Robert and William Craig in 1837, the first Jefferson Township pioneers." The same source states that John Davis, John Snider, James Ferguson, and Levi Young arrived in 1838. Regardless of who was first, they were all "adventurous spirits who reasoned that, despite all obstacles that confronted them, the land was good, and would eventually furnish homes and farms for themselves and their children."

Apparently the little cluster of crude log buildings was called Bee Creek for a brief time, since the first post office was established under that name on September 26, 1846, with Levi Young as postmaster. Perhaps that name was retained even after the infant village underwent its first sale of town lots in 1846. The credit for the founding of the town goes to John Craig, John Odgen, and J. R. LeFever, for it was they who "laid it out" in 1846. By 1850, when the settlement was formally platted, its name was officially listed as Ossian.

The origin of the name is still not entirely clear. That the town was named for the legendary Celtic poet, Ossian, is of course not disputed, but just who came up with the idea of honoring him in this fashion has not been recorded. It is known

49

Early street scene of Ossian with the Methodist Church in the background.

that Craig was born in Scotland and that his family was acquainted with the poet Robert Burns. Many families in the area also traced their ancestry to Scotland, which may account for the choice of the name.

Plans for a new plank road between Fort Wayne and Bluffton, and the organization of the first Ossian school also took place in 1850, and the little village was on its way. By 1854, a Captain Karnes had been hired to engineer a log bridge over Eight Mile Creek; primitive roads to the east and west were not long in coming, and the clearing of village lots continued at a steady pace. By 1861 the population of the little hamlet had reached approximately 200, and this was due, in large part, to the presence of these improvements. Everyone traveling on the plank road with a horse and wagon of any sort had to pay the toll, which was collected by William Craig at the toll gate situated on South Main Street, but foot passengers could use the plank road for free. When a wagon's wheels did not hit both planks on the road, water splashed up and the mud flew.

In 1854, Mr. Chapman ran the local store and took care of the mail, which came twice a week from Bluffton or Fort Wayne by means of a stagecoach driven by Wilson Deam. There were only two streets, Main and Mill, at that time. Flour and cornmeal for the village store often came from as far away as Pennvillle, Indiana (called Camden at one time).

COMING OF THE RAILROAD

The appearance of the long-awaited railroad north and south through Wells County was a boon to every hamlet along its route. Genuine prosperity was evidenced by the number of frame houses erected in Ossian in the next few years. Since the presence of log cabins came to signify backward pioneer conditions, people couldn't pull them down fast enough.

Thanks to the completion of the Fort Wayne, Cincinnati & Louisville Railroad, various industries began to spring up in Ossian. One of the first, a stave and heading factory built by Carey and Baker in 1870, burned in 1872 and was rebuilt the same year. It was then purchased by H. Hatfield in 1876. In 1882, E. Nimmons became the owner, developing a booming business shipping barrel staves and circled headings to the Standard Oil Company. In its heyday it employed 100 men. Koons, Milligan, and Glass built a sawmill in 1872. It was later enlarged by Koons, Beaty, and Doan. Wood products in general were important Wells county exports, but the clearing of the land for agriculture rapidly exhausted the supply of raw material. By about 1900, sawmills began to have less importance due to the great amount of logging that had taken place.

Based on the idea that farmers in the area could be convinced to turn to dairying and thus ensure a steady supply of milk, C. W. Eastman, J. W. Craig, and W. C. Hatfield founded the Ossian Creamery. At first it was a pronounced success; however, the agricultural community became more enamored with raising hogs and cattle, because they could more quickly realize a profit. The locally famous Climax Butter melted away with the demise of the creamery.

The first flour mill was built in 1864 by James Gorrell and John Brown, after which time it was serviced by many owners. It burned down twice and was rebuilt each time. Around the turn of the century, when owned by Woodward and Rupright, it had two runs of burrs for wheat, one for middlings, and one for corn. There was an ashery at 201 Mill Street, where the powdery gray/white residue from burning lumber was converted to lye, which was used for soap and other household products. The ashes were leached with water, which was then evaporated in boiling kettles until the residue became stiff and hard. The product was also known as black salt and was used for seasoning.

As early as 1890, T. A. Doan and the Hatfield firm built an elevator near the Ossian track switch, and this for a time served local needs. In 1890 the firm changed hands and William Beatty became the partner of Doan. Business was slow at first, but farmers soon began to realize that it paid them to sell locally. By 1899 a large corncrib was built, equipped with a power sheller and other apparatus.

Every community has its growing pains, and Ossian was no exception. During the decade of the 1890s, the town experienced a minor crisis in matters of public morality. Growth associated with the prosperity of the sawmill and the stave factory had brought workingmen to town whose recreational pursuits included hard drinking in saloons and reckless gambling wherever the opportunity afforded, and this was looked upon with alarm by the churches and the local temperance society. The Ossian correspondent of the *Bluffton Chronicle*, who wrote a long and detailed column for the paper each week concerning the noteworthy happenings in the village, reported the mounting tension between the two groups.

Store in Ossian around 1900. Note the hitching post in the foreground and wooden sidewalks.

Local citizens posing around Sharp's Hardware located at the southwest corner of what is today Jefferson Street (Indiana 1) and Mill Street.

Poker was apparently the game of choice among the young roisterers, and it was said that games were being played on Sundays in buggy sheds, ice houses, and barns around town, and when the weather favored, players were also congregating on the railroad bridge or in the adjacent woods. Also interspersed among the usual social notes concerning the comings and goings of prominent citizens were stories of barroom brawls, runaway youths, vandalism, and burglaries by brazen safe-crackers.

In an attempt to halt this scandalous march toward perdition, the temperance group invited Mason Long, the notorious reformed Fort Wayne gambler and self-professed ex-drunkard, to town to speak on the evils of wagering and tippling. Arriving in a "magnificent equipage" and accompanied by a "splendid quartette of singers," Long spoke convincingly to a large crowd on the main street. But apparently Long's eloquence had little effect on the rowdy youths to whom it had been directed, for only a few weeks later local toughs attempted to break up a regular meeting of the temperance society, to the consternation of many in the town.

Being connected to both Fort Wayne and Bluffton by means of the railroad, Ossian frequently felt aggrieved by visits made by unruly travelers from those places, who were attracted to the saloons in town. Vagrants, too, plagued the picnic grounds, congregating there and even spending the nights sleeping under the stars. The railroad was undoubtedly the source of such unwelcome visitors, but the presence of the nearby saloons didn't help.

The old mill in Ossian owned by Woodward and Rupright in 1914.

In 1894, the saloon problem was vigorously attacked by the leaders of the town, which had recently been incorporated, by imposing heavy taxes on such establishments. The last one closed its doors on June 13 of that year.

Although gambling was almost always associated with the operation of a racetrack, most of the community approved the building of a track on the outskirts of town in the early 1890s. It was successfully operated for several years, apparently without exciting a great deal of unfavorable comment.

An "opera house" was also present on the second floor of one of the town's business buildings, and although traveling theater troupes were often criticized for their lax morals and the raciness of some of their productions, the opera house was a welcome addition to the little town's short list of amenities.

The excitement generated by the oil and gas boom in the southern townships led speculators to drill all over the area, even in the northernmost reaches of the county. Ossian was caught up in the natural-gas fever in the summer of 1891 when a test well was sunk near town. A large crowd of spectators was on hand to witness the proceedings, and loud cheers erupted when a 70-foot-high geyser of salt water shot out of the drill casing, followed by a burst of gas (ignited by a kitchen match), and then another column of water. It may have been dramatic to watch, but the developers were disappointed, and the rigging was dismantled a short time later. No more was said about a gas field for Ossian.

For many years around the turn of the century, Ossian was renowned for its excellent brass band, as well as for its outstanding choral music. The *Chronicle* was of the opinion that this was due to the presence in town of several very gifted

Charles Goshorn and Raymond Hendry in front of the popular city lunch room where local residents enjoyed the blue plate special with ice cream for dessert.

music teachers, whose efforts had resulted in making Ossian a place where nearly every household was subject to the "elevating influence of this beautiful art."

AT THE TURN OF THE CENTURY

The Ossian of 1900 was a pleasant place indeed, a far cry from the primitive, malarial swampland of 1846. The turn of the century saw a tidy prosperous town of nearly a thousand residents. The streets were lined with frame houses in the handsome Queen Anne style, with intricate embellishments, bay windows, and decorative scrolled brackets. The town's thoroughfares were all neatly graveled, and there were sturdy wooden sidewalks and shade trees everywhere. Various business ventures filled every need of the community. Businesses were represented by H. Hatfield, who ran the general store; Anderson Morton, who offered dry goods; J. H. Hoover and Bell & Davis, druggists; Henry Kreigh, grocer; William Quackenbush, baker; Ellsworth Salisbury who combined hardware with being an undertaker; Earl and Harvey Spence, who had the wagon shop; Stine and Son, and Stoine and McCollum, blacksmiths; Marcellus Donaldson, who owned the shoe shop; and Mary Vincore and Mrs. Willmington, the town's milliners.

Professional services were also not lacking, with J. I. Metts, A. H. Metts, and M. N. Newman serving as physicians, and John Chalfant providing legal services.

In later years the Heyerly brothers established a bakery at the corner of Main

Eve's Restaurant, an Ossian landmark for years, was the meeting place where one could grouse about the latest Ossian gossip while enjoying breakfast, lunch, or supper, or just a snack and a cup of coffee.

The Interurban provided a convenient way to travel north to Fort Wayne or points south including Bluffton and Muncie. This view is of the interurban station in 1917.

Street (now known as Jefferson) and Mill Street. The bakery has been in continuous operation since 1931, with people traveling from all over the area to obtain Heyerley's famous rolls, cakes, and breads.

SCHOOLS

Organized in 1850, the first school in the town of Ossian was taught by Robert M. Johnson in an old log kitchen of one of the early settlers. It was located near the site of what was later the residence of Walter Craig. In 1851 the first public school, a small, crudely built log structure, was erected near what was later Dr. Metts's office. The first schoolmaster, Johnson, was followed by other early instructors, including Jacob J. Todd, Maggie Hawkins, and A. B. Cartwright. A small frame building succeeded the log structure. It was replaced in the 1860s by a frame two-story building under the trusteeship of Dr. J. I. Metts, who served in that capacity for twenty-one years. Jennie Sterling was the first teacher to institute grade arrangements in the schools.

A two-story brick structure was erected in 1878 at the cost of $5,000 when James Gorrell was trustee. Professor P. A. Allen, who would later serve as Bluffton's superintendent of schools, was the first principal in the first brick schoolhouse. After being occupied for twenty years, it was condemned in 1898, and two years later it was rebuilt as a modern schoolhouse of eight rooms.

David H. Swaim, successor to Allen as principal, was influential in grading and organizing the Ossian School. The school grew and was incorporated as part of the Northern Wells School System when schools were consolidated in Wells County in 1961.

Northern Wells Community Schools' original school board was composed of Clyde Barners, Darrel Gilbert, William Borror, Jr., Rex Shutt, and Walter Speheger, and the offices of the school corporation were located in Ossian. Today, Ossian houses a modern elementary school, recently enlarged and remodeled at the site of the former Ossian High School, which serves students from kindergarten through grade five.

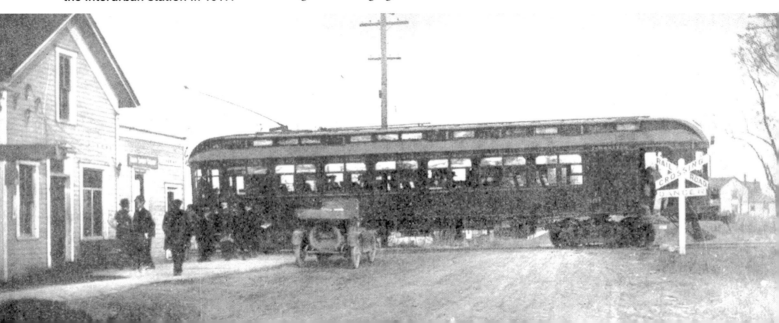

Ossian was first introduced to the telephone when the Bell Telephone Company put in a station and a long distance line in 1882. Then James H. Keefer entered both the publishing and communication fields. In 1880 he began issuing the *News*, which he continued until 1914, and in February 1896, he built a private telephone line between his newspaper office and residence. Others soon became aware of the advantages of communicating between the railroad, the livery-stable, and other business establishments, and thirteen individuals entered into an agreement with Mr. Keefer to put up a "series line" for local needs. In the summer of 1899, the Central Union Telephone Company made their agents, Roe Brothers, a proposition to put in an exchange system allowing each subscriber the privilege of long distance communication.

Although Ossian has had the benefit of a local newspaper for many years, the first one established there in the 1880s, *The Ossian Weekly Telephone*, lasted only a few months. Following the demise of Keefer's *News*, the *Ossian Journal* was founded in April 1914, by B. F. Sprunger. For many years it was published by Edward Peck, who in the last decade sold it to the *News-Banner* in Bluffton. It is still published three times a week as a subsidiary of the *News-Banner*.

The Farmers State Bank was founded in November 1912, by E. W. Dyar, president; L. M. Springer, vice-president; and A. A. Melching, cashier. While banks throughout the county were failing, the Ossian Farmers State Bank stayed in business until 1932, when it was reorganized as the Ossian State Bank. Today the Ossian State Bank is a significant financial institution in Wells County with a branch in Bluffton and widespread interests throughout the area.

In October 1939, the Bluffton-Wells County Public Library Board of Trustees chose to enrich the knowledge of rural Wells County by providing better service to its citizens by using a

Paving the streets of Ossian did much to improve the quality of life in the town. The exact date of paving is not known, but probably did not occur until around 1915–1920.

The public school in Ossian which replaced the first brick school house after it was condemned.

The Wells County Public Library Bookmobile which served Ossian prior to the establishment of a branch library.

traveling library. This library was in the form of a twenty foot-long semi-trailer made especially for that purpose and pulled by a pickup truck. The unit was designed and built locally by Sylvan Tonner. Originally, the Bookmobile, as it was called, visited Lancaster School, Ossian, Tocsin, Craigville, and Vera Cruz on Thursdays of each week.

By 1979, the public library provided, for its patrons, a self-contained vehicle constructed on a recreational vehicle chassis, which offered a variety of materials and story hours for children. The demand in Ossian was such that the Bookmobile was spending a full day at Ossian, and it was obvious that greater service in the form of a Branch Library was not only desired but truly needed.

The Ossian Branch Library, which was first located in a store-front leased from Charles Hissem on Jefferson Street, served the community well for several years. At the same time, a branch had also been established in Zanesville. Community demands and needs for library service continued to increase in the Ossian community, and the branch soon outgrew its store-front home. It was then decided to purchase the Hunter home at 207 North Jefferson Street and also the adjoining service station and property on Mill Street. At the same time the Zanesville branch was closed because of the low demand in the area. The Hunter home filled the needs adequately for several years, but had the disadvantage of not being handicap accessible with the only available meeting room being located on the second floor. Insufficient storage space for books was also a problem, as was the lack of story-hour facilities for the school and nursery school children who visited weekly.

The need for greater and more suitable space and savings from the main library building project provided the opportunity for the construction of a new 3,750 square foot library branch at the cost of $250,000 with no additional cost to the taxpayer. The new structure, handicap accessible with adequate storage for materials, and containing a separate meeting room for community use, was opened in November 1994.

Another institution currently significant to the community is the Ossian Fire Department, which began as long ago as 1895, when the village board of trustees bought a chemical engine for protection against fire, since the water supply was limited to a series of cisterns or reservoirs placed at strategic points within the corporate limits. Early attempts to form hook and ladder units failed, and many homes and businesses were lost to fire. Today the Ossian Fire Department not only serves all of Jefferson Township but also provides Emergency Medical Services for the northern part of Wells County.

EARLY CHURCHES IN OSSIAN

The religious community is always an integral part of the ongoing strength of an area. Ossian early on was the location of many churches that are still in existence today. The earliest was the Presbyterian Church, organized in 1840 at the home of Adam Hatfield by the Rev. Isaac A. Ogden with thirty charter members. It was first known as the Pleasant Ridge Presbyterian Church, and the first meeting place was in a log building about two and one-half miles southwest of the village. Later a plain frame building was built in 1858 during the ministry of the Rev. W. M. Donaldson. The name was then changed to the Ossian Presbyterian Church. During the pastorate of the Rev. E. P. Gilchrish in 1902 the present substantial brick church was built.

Methodism took root in Jefferson Township as early as 1848. The Ossian Circuit was organized two years later as a part of the Saint Mary's Mission, which included all the territory south of Fort Wayne and north of the Wabash River. The Ossian Society was organized in 1851 and worshipped in the schoolhouse and various private homes until 1853, when the first church was completed. The Rev. J. W. Foughty was the first class leader. Today these congregations, along with the Nazarene Church, remain a viable force in the community.

Two churches existed historically but have since disbanded. The Christian Church, which was organized at the schoolhouse in 1881, had ceased having regular services by 1886. The Bethel United Brethern Church was dedicated in August 1882, but had only a membership of about fifty in 1917.

CLUBS AND FRATERNAL ORGANIZATIONS IN OSSIAN

Around 1900, Ossian boasted more social organizations than any other town in Wells County with the exception of Bluffton, having four secret societies and four organizations for women. The Ossian Lodge No. 297, Free and Accepted Masons, met under dispensation in September 1893, with charter members John P. Nash, E. Covert, B. F. Taylor, William Beatty, J. I. Metts, Joseph Kreigh, and Thomas Vail. The lodge room was destroyed by fire in 1877, leaving the society

A disastrous fire destroyed the entire Hatfield block May 27, 1908. It pointed out the need for better fire protection.

The Ossian Presbyterian orchestra was one of several serious musical groups in the community in the 1920s.

The Knights of Pythias Lodge in 1904 on what was then Main Street and is today Jefferson Street. Part of the Hatfield block, it was destroyed by fire four years later.

bankrupt, since there was no insurance. With the help of neighboring lodges the group survived. In addition, Chapter 166 of the Order of Eastern Star was organized on January 25, 1895, with thirty members and Jacob J. Todd of Bluffton as installing officer. Miss Lizzie J. N. Johnston was Worthy Matron, and J. C. Hatfield was Worthy Patron.

Castle Hall Lodge, Knights of Pythias, was instituted with thirty-four charter members February 4, 1892, by George W. Grimes of the Bluffton lodge. The Knights of Pythias were recognized for their charitable work in the community. The Garland Temple No. 118 of Rathbone Sisters, the sister organization of the Knights of Pythias, was instituted December 31, 1894, by Mary Lipkey of Bluffton. The International Order of Odd Fellows was instituted November 12, 1895, by District Deputy Grand Master W. D. Fitch, with twelve charter members. Rebecca Lodge, the sister organization of the Odd Fellows, was granted a charter on March 21, 1898, with fifteen charter members. The oldest club still in existence today is the Sargasso Literary Club, which was formed in 1900. Strict rules concerning the dress code and book reviews have been relaxed over the years.

OSSIAN TODAY

Today, Ossian and northern Wells County are the fastest growing areas in the county. Just within the last decade, the town has completed a substantial economic development. With its close proximity to the Fort Wayne metropolitan area, it is an ideal spot for those who wish to live away from the hustle and bustle of the city and yet have access to its attractions.

K. of P. Lodge,
instituted Feb. 4, 1892,
Ossian, Indiana.

Hatfield Block. Destroyed by Fire, 27, 1908, 12:45 A. M

The exponential economic growth in the Ossian Industrial Park in the past decade can be attributed to the efforts of the Ossian Economic Development Corporation. Ed Peck and Gene Donoghy were instrumental in the formation of the Ossian Economic Development Corporation and Edward Goetz came on board in 1985 as the Executive Director. In December of that year, Johnson Controls announced the construction of a plant to supply seat sets for the General Motors Truck plant in Fort Wayne. Lt. Governor John Mutz; State Representative Jeff Espich; John Daly, chairman of the board of the Hoover Universal (owner of Johnson Controls); and local dignitaries were present at the ground breaking on September 4, 1985. At the dinner to establish the Ossian Industrial Park, $24,000 was raised in pledges for the initial development. The economic growth of Ossian was ignited and has been fueled with many successes since that date.

Karen's Kitchens (now called Brothers Bakery) resulted from a contact made at the Northeast Indiana Development Conference in Pokagon in June 1987. In 1989, Bob and Kathy Boling built Precision Machinery, which was later purchased and expanded by John Roembke. This was followed by Thermatron Manufacturing, built and operated by Milt Gerber, for the manufacture of paper pulping machines for cellulose insulation. The plant was later sold to Michael Gerber who has since expanded the operation. Acme Waste Systems needed a maintenance building and was another addition to the Industrial Park. John and Mack Perkins then decided to move their precision machine component operation, JRP Precision Machinery, to Ossian in 1991. The second national company to locate in Ossian was the Walbro Corporation, and it has expanded several times since its construction. Melching Machine moved to the Industrial Park from another Ossian location when greater space was needed. The Industrial Park expanded to the west side of the Norfolk and Southern railroad when Vision Scan and Dave Hissem purchased land there. More than 700 jobs were created through this decade of extraordinary economic growth, ensuring that Ossian will not become another promising Wells County community that disintegrates to little more than a crossroads.

Were they here to see it, the earliest settlers of little "Bee Creek," would have every reason to be proud of their many accomplishments. The "howling wilderness" of the 1840s has been tamed at great cost. Today their descendants, when they celebrate their annual "Ossian Days" festival each fall, can look about them and see comforts and conveniences that were totally undreamed of back in those first "Ossian Days" of 1846.

—B. Elliott

Everyone loves a parade and especially the Knights of Pythias Band, which is leading the lodge members on parade in Ossian about the turn of the century.

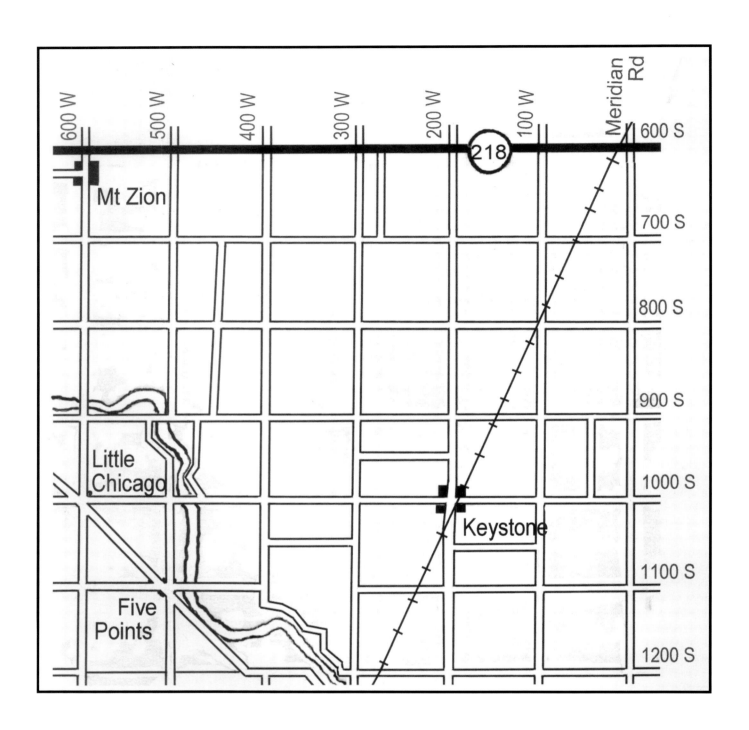

CHESTER TOWNSHIP

3

Most records agree that the first settlers of Chester Township were Henry McCullick, Newton Putnam, Alpheus T. Stevens, Wilson Brown, Thomas Blunt, and Joseph Blunt who came in 1836; John Lancaster, Jonas Jarrett, and Benjamin Starr in 1837; Issac Lancaster, Alexander Walker, John McCullick, and J. Brotherton in 1838; Levi Phillips, Franklin Spaulding, and James Jordon in 1839; Samuel Rice, and Thomas Hulet in 1840; and Joseph H. McGrath and Sewell Snow in 1841.

The Miami Indians present when settlers arrived in Chester township were friendly and peaceful, offering no recorded problems, as was also the case in other parts of the county. A creek that empties into the Salamonie River in southern Chester Township, and extending upstream into southern Nottingham Township, is named "Scuffle Creek." There is no origin of the name recorded except the first government land survey party, in Wells County in 1822, recorded this name for the creek in their plotting. It was also on the banks of this creek where the first commercial oil well was drilled in Indiana.

When Henry McCullick came with his family from Athens County, Ohio, he came as far as Muncie by a road previously cut; from Muncie he had to cut his own road. Arriving in October 1835, they stayed with the Thomas Blunt family until February 1836, when they moved into their own log cabin with a clapboard roof and a puncheon floor. Puncheon floors were common in many of the cabins. Split logs, with the face smoothed with hand tools were an improvement over dirt floors. McCullick was claimed by one writer as the best hunter in this part of the state, having killed seven panthers and more deer and other game than any other man in Wells County. It was said that another Chester settler, John Lancaster, had killed 500 deer.

TOWNSHIP ORGANIZED

Chester Township was not organized until 1841, four years after Wells County was organized. It was first included by the County Commissioners as a part of Jackson Township when it was organized in September 1837. On March 1, 1841, the first election was held at the home of Jonas Jarrett to formally organize the township. Trustees elected were Jonas Jarrett, Henry McCullick, and Joseph Hulet; Newton Putnam, clerk-treasurer; James Jordon, justice of the peace; Thomas Hulet, constable; and John Brotherton, supervisor. The meeting resulted in dividing the township into four road districts and four school districts. The first road was known as the Huntington Road, and the second was known as the McCullick Road.

Early settlers traveled with their family and all of their possessions. Leaving civilization and going to a new home in the wilderness was a long tedious trip over a poorly marked and dangerous trail.

Arriving in Wells County, the family's first need was a cabin for protection from the weather. Trees were felled, trimmed, and notched to lay up the sidewalls.

PIONEER LIFE

The first chore of the settlers who arrived in Chester Township was to provide shelters for their families. A temporary shelter of boughs and brush would soon be replaced by a cabin, raised in only one day with the help of neighbors who assembled for the "house raising." The first days in the new cabin were often spent with an open fire in the center of the room and a hole in the roof to exhaust the smoke, until the fireplace and chimney were completed. Often the cabin would be well ventilated until the space between the log walls was chinked and daubed with clay. The puncheon floor was hewn smooth on the upper side—quite substantial and solid. Many cabins had a front porch. The chimney was made of sticks and clay, the fireplace and hearth of local stones. Bed frames were made by inserting poles in augured holes in the wall and fixing legs to the ends. Cross-members were tied or pegged in place. Utensils and tools were hung on the walls and a rifle and powder horn hung above the door on forked cleats.

One early writer stated that "to save light and fuel, and for general convenience, we arranged to have our kitchen, dining room, and sitting room, all in one room. And when the occasion demanded it, we converted this room into a shoe shop, a corn grating shop, a spinning and weaving room, and sometimes used it for a gun shop and axe handle factory."

Chief articles of the pioneer diet were hominy, cornbread, venison, pork, honey, beans, pumpkin, turkey, and prairie chicken. Wheat bread, tea, coffee, and fruit were luxuries not to be indulged in except on special occasions.

All of the clothing was homespun. If a young man would appear in a suit of store clothes it would only be for his wedding.

Before staple items became available in Bluffton, flour and salt could only be obtained by an arduous journey to Muncie, Fort Wayne, or even Henry County. The first settlers made these trips without the advantage of trails or roads. The only bridges were those built by the pioneers by felling trees across the river. The trips required several days, and if rains came, the swollen rivers and rain-soaked marsh areas lengthened the trip to weeks.

Chester Township in its early days was primitive and sparsely populated. It was known as a haunt for wolves and "panthers," and people said even its water was of poor quality. But the soil was rich, and the area's potential for solid prosperity was apparent to the hard-working men and women who settled there and began very laboriously to clear the land.

Work was arduous but the ingenuous settlers were able to combine fun with the work. "Quilting bees," "corn huskings," "apple parings," "log rollings," and "house raisings" were festivities enjoyed with a carnival spirit. The events included an abundance of food, dancing, and sometimes the "finding of a red ear of corn." It was at these "husking bees" that young men met their future wives. Any lad who husked an ear of corn and found a red ear could claim a kiss. And many were the red ears that were husked repeatedly!

Great times were had when the fall butchering season arrived. Families would gather to put up enough meat to last the winter. Early on, wild hogs, once domestic swine that had been left behind, or had escaped from their owners and became wild and vicious, were caught and butchered. Surplus meat was packed with salt in barrels and sent to market. The cooper trade was therefore profitable during those times. Tenderloins, spare ribs, the pig's head and feet were not considered of much value.

A wolf-chase or snake-killing was a delight for the men and boys who enjoyed the chase. The wolf-chase was conducted with elaborate signals and rules. The men formed a large circle and closed in while the dogs were held in check until a signal was given for the dogs to be turned loose for the kill. Snakes were usually killed in large numbers in the spring when they were out sunning themselves. The men sealed the hole to their den and killed them wholesale with spades, mattocks, clubs, and crowbars. The fattest were made into an oil extract, and the skins were saved as a specifics for rheumatism.

The boys had good times hunting bees' nests by tracing the flight of a bee to find its hive. When a hive was found, usually in a hollow tree, the tree was marked for cutting the following September, when several gallons of honey might be taken from a single tree.

Chester resident Benjamin Starr, arriving in Bluffton on a business trip, learned he had a letter from back east with two cents postage due. Having no money, and unable to find others with money, Starr earned the two cents by spending a half day cleaning out a dug well for Squire Hale, thus saving a return trip to claim the letter.

DRAINAGE

Construction of ditches for land drainage was an important early step for the new township. Natural drainage of the generally flat land was inadequate to provide tillable land. Low areas were wet and slow in drying in the spring. At first the natural waterways were enlarged by the cooperation of families living along the routes. In 1876, Joseph Burns et. al. petitioned for a drainage ditch which would become the first established by law in Wells County. The Burns ditch was 27,700 feet in length, constructed at a cost of $1789.60 or twelve and a half cents per cubic yard.

CHESTER SCHOOLS

The first school was in section 36, the southeast corner of the township, taught by Miss Eliza A. Groves, the first lady teacher in Wells County. By 1870 there were ten schools, located every two miles, except for the Keystone school. The schoolhouses were frame buildings, later abandoned in favor of brick around 1890.

Splitting wood was a back-breaking, never ending job for the early settlers. Firewood for cooking, heating water, and keeping the cabin warm was necessary for survival.

Spinning wool fiber into yarn was but one of many tasks for the pioneer housewife. Besides the care of the home and children, the wife frequently helped with planting and harvesting.

These one-room schoolhouses, once a feature of the American landscape, are now a part of folklore. Stories of the hardships and discomforts, as well as the boisterous games, spelling bees, inspiring teachers, and lasting friendships that characterized such rural neighborhood schools, are now only found in books and sometimes on television. Fortunately, Chester Township has in its midst a sturdy historic relic from those times. The old Five Points School, also known in its day as Chester Township School Number Nine, is still standing in its original location at the point at which the Jeff Road and County Roads 600 West and 1000 South intersect. Its name derives from the fact that from the center of the intersection, roads lead off in five directions, or points on the compass. The Salamonie River is nearby and the countryside is gently rolling and attractive.

The school was unusual in having two stories, with the second story used for a Grange Hall, rather than as a classroom. A one-story, single room wooden structure had occupied the spot prior to 1876, but in that year the old schoolhouse was demolished and the present brick structure was erected on the one-acre site. The story goes that the Goodin family donated one-half acre for the school that was originally built, and that the Spaulding family, whose farm lay on the western side of the school ground, donated the second half-acre when it was decided to combine the Grange Hall with the school facility. The Grange, an organization devoted to promoting the welfare of farmers through political and social action, flourished in the 1870s throughout the nation.

As was usual in those days, water for drinking and washing-up was drawn from an open dug well to one side of the building. Toilet facilities were of the outside variety, and heating the large room was accomplished by means of wood stoves. Fuel supplies were easily replenished by the older boys, as the schoolhouse was surrounded by thick woods on three sides in the earliest times.

The school grounds at Five Points were used for a community fair in the first years. Exhibits of crafts, handiwork, and horticulture were featured, as well as championship livestock, with organized games for young and old alike livening up matters periodically. The fair was eventually moved to Montpelier, however, where there was a race track to accommodate horse fanciers, as well as larger buildings in which to display the agricultural exhibits and hold dances.

In addition to the usual "readin', writin', and 'rithmetic" one expected in a one-room school, Five Points also offered debating contests, "cipherin'" matches, singing schools, and spelling bees. On occasion, community dances would be held there in the evenings. It was clearly a community gathering place for the people of southwestern Chester Township.

One former student of the school, Mrs. Bessie Spaulding Shadle, writing in 1959, remembered that during the oil-boom days in the early part of the twentieth century, the school was let out when drillers were ready to "shoot" a well on the Goodin property, presumably as a precaution against some untoward incident involving the nitroglycerine used to start the oil flowing. She remembered, too, that the teachers at Five Points were well-respected by their students and that "no crime ever came out of this school."

When the first consolidation of township schools occurred in 1920, the old Five Points school was closed forever, but the building continued to be used until 1928 by an organization calling itself "The Horse Thief Detective Association." While there may have been a need for such a quasi-vigilante group at one time in the earlier days of Wells County's history, by the late 1920s it was undoubtedly a purely social venture.

The long history of the Five Points School and its building has been preserved by the non-profit group, "The Five Points School Association." The group is restoring the building, and establishing an historical exhibit and meeting hall there. Backers hope that the old school, so closely associated with the history of Chester Township, will serve as a focal point, gathering place, and tourist attraction for the area.

The Keystone School was erected in 1896 under the term of Trustee Frank Risley. Will S. Van Horn was the first principal. Teachers, in addition to Mr. Van Horn, were Jennie Macy and Julia L. Ady. Wilman Thrush followed Van Horn as principal, and then A. R. Huyette, who later became county superintendent of schools. The superintendent's required visits to all of the county's schools was by horse and buggy.

In 1923 a consolidated school building was built in the center of the township, with all pupils brought to the school by buses. Some Jackson Township pupils were brought to the Chester school until Jackson built their Jackson Center School in 1937.

Professor P. A. Allen, identified with the progress of education in Wells County, told of early school teaching. The prevailing idea was "no licken', no larnin' ", as a gad was held in the teacher's right hand while in his left he supported his book, pen, or slate. Daily lessons began with the smaller boys and girls standing individually at the teacher's knee, saying the ABC's. Then came the first and second spelling classes, and the second, third, and fourth reading classes. While reciting, pupils stood in line near the wall opposite the teacher's split-bottomed chair. One or two books answered the need of the scholars, who had to take their turn. And woe to the teacher who refused to work a sum, or pronounce a hard word. After all, he was paid one dollar a day to know how to work those sums and spell those hard words.

At the close of the day, a prepared lesson was spelled. Starting at the head of the class, the pupils spelled and pronounced the words by syllables. The success-

Going to the mill to have corn and wheat ground was a long trip through the forest and sometimes across rain-swollen rivers.

Spring planting was done by hand. Here corn was being planted a kernel at a time. Many hours in the field were needed, and "many hands made light work."

ful spellers went to the head of the class, receiving a "head mark" if he was still there when the class dismissed.

Spelling bees were popular evening social features. Debating societies were also featured with all of the fervor and combat of the halls of Congress. Among questions debated were: "Resolved, that the dog is of more value to man than his gun;" "that cattle are of greater use to man than the horse;" and "that war is a greater evil than intemperance." Township libraries were established in the homes of the trustees in about 1854, with books available to everyone, particularly those interested in debating. Box socials were held to furnish books for the township and school libraries.

CHURCHES ESTABLISHED

The pioneers were God-fearing people who soon organized to meet the need for a house of worship. The first meetings were held in family or neighborhood groups, in private homes. The United Brethren Church was constructed in 1855. It was a hewn log building, 24 by 30 feet. The Christian Church was erected in 1864, followed by the Chester Center Union Church, a frame building seating four hundred persons, in 1870. The Ebenezer Baptist Church was organized during this period, and in 1883, the Methodist Protestant Church was organized. Following this period, the Society of Friends, or Quakers, had a church in Keystone, and their burial ground, which dates from 1880 is still a point of local interest just north of the village on County Road 200 West.

OIL DISCOVERY

Chester Township was in the midst of Wells County's oil boom territory that extended into both Nottingham and Jackson townships, with a few wells drilled in Liberty Township. There was feverish activity in leasing land in the late 1880s when oil was discovered. A well drilled by the Northern Indiana Oil Company on the D. A. Bryson farm, near Keystone in June 1890, was the first commercially viable oil well in Indiana. Wells County was the largest oil producing county in the state at a time when the Midwest was the primary producer of petroleum. Scores of drilling outfits were in operation at the height of the boom and at the close of the century there were nearly a thousand producing wells in the county, some producing several hundred barrels of oil daily. In some instances, a well would pay for itself within the first few days of operation. The average depth of the wells was approximately 1000 feet.

An October 22, 1891, newspaper article stated: "No less than 25 oil derricks can be counted standing at the crossroads at Nottingham, and most of the wells are paying." Ordinarily, if an area was found to be a good producer, there would be a well in about every ten acres. In September 1892, a well was reported producing 600 barrels of oil in 24 hours.

The oil field was at its peak before the days of the automobile and truck.

Teamsters transported drilling machinery, pumping equipment, well casings, pipe for pipelines, etc. Pumping stations dotted the oil fields, and the crude oil was pumped into tanks to be gauged and then put into pipelines to be transported to supply stations or the refineries of large oil companies.

As oil production began to decline in the early 1900s with the exhaustion of the oil pools, wells were abandoned, casings pulled, and wells plugged. Oil men moved on to newly discovered fields in Kansas, Oklahoma, and Texas.

CHESTER TOWNS

Luther Twibell, a Virginian who had come to Indiana with his parents and had lived for a time in Blackford County, was the founder of Keystone. When he married at the age of twenty in 1841, he and his bride emigrated to Wells County and purchased eighty acres in Section 23 of Chester Township, which was then mainly a trackless wilderness of dark forest and swampland.

Luther immediately began the back-breaking task of clearing his land, after having built his small log cabin in only one day. At first the floor of the little dwelling was of earth, the table and bed were made by pounding stakes in the ground and placing clapboards on top of them, and instead of a regular fireplace, there was a temporary fire pit in the middle of the room. A conventional hearth and chimney followed soon after. In later years the house was locally famous for having in it the first cast-iron cook stove in the vicinity, purchased by the young Twibell sons, William and David, with money earned from a special plot set aside for them by their father.

Luther Twibell platted the village of Keystone in 1872, on a portion of his farm. It was apparent that the Fort Wayne-to-Muncie railroad (the Norfolk & Southern railroad today) would be a growing concern and that commercial possibilities were opening all along the route, and the route would border a portion of his land. After an exciting contest to select a name, the town was named Keystone in honor of Pennsylvania, the Keystone State, which was the birthplace of his wife. Two additions were added to the original plat in 1874. By 1875, Keystone was listed as having a post office.

Neighbors joined together in the fall harvest season. Corn stalks were cut and put in shocks to dry. As the winter set in, husking bees were events that brought the pioneer families together for work and fun.

The village made considerable progress for several years. At various times it had two or three general stores, blacksmith shops, a warehouse, saw mills, a drugstore, and one or two physicians. Keystone was the gathering place for the neighborhood when the farm work was done, or bad weather prevailed. The men congregated at the general store. This was a scene found in every Wells County town. Many hours were spent around the wood burning stove, exchanging news, telling stories, and playing checkers. Many still have memories of those who would bite off a "chaw" of plug tobacco. The spitting of tobacco juice into a nearby bucket was an unsanitary act repeated frequently by the "regulars."

The blacksmith shop played a very important part in the life of every farmer. Some had their own forge for emergency repairs, but the village smithy was indispensable. Here you could get new shoes made for your horses and have them shod. Plowshares could be made and sharpened. Tools of any description could be made and repaired at the "smithy."

The discovery of oil in southern Wells County in the 1890s initiated a boom period for Keystone as well. Oil was the magic power that doubled its population. Buildings were at a premium and new ones were quickly erected.

The oil production suffered because of a high sulfur content reducing its value, and the early methods of over-production curtailed output. The bubble burst about 1905 when Keystone's growth declined. The gradual loss of oil revenue and its derivative income was a set-back, but by 1910 Keystone seemingly recovered. In 1914 Keystone had three general stores, a meat market, a blacksmith shop, a jewelry shop, a hardware store, and a restaurant. The presence of the Union Traction Company's interurban helped, and the agricultural boom associated with World War I, beginning in late 1916, continued the prosperity. Agriculture continued to support the town, along with Cline's large grain elevator. In addition, in 1917 the Keystone Bank was organized. However, the agricultural depression that began in 1921 soon wiped out those gains. The bustling little town began to shrink in size as businesses closed their doors forever or moved their operations to larger communities.

During the depression years of the 1930s Keystone sported a horseshoe court and an adjoining croquet court, both providing heated games for spectators and players alike. Teams from other county towns participated in the action. The croquet court featured wood sideboards with a carefully maintained, perfectly level sand surface. Mallets were hand-made with care to give the owner the best advantage in the contests. Johnson's General Store was at the corner, and "up the hill" was Feltt's General Store with the Woodmen's Lodge on the second floor. At one time, the second floor had a roller skating rink. Outdoor movies were enjoyed free-of-charge during summer evenings when the pictures were projected on the side of Clifford Twibell's Garage building. During that period, the town had a second garage and a barber shop.

The only other towns were Mt. Zion and Little Chicago, both on the Chester-Jackson Township line. Neither town was platted, but Mt. Zion is still on the map, while Little Chicago, with only one general store, disappeared in the 1920s.

—P. Bender

A gun was a valuable possession that provided game to feed the family. Many pioneers became expert marksmen. Many of the women learned to shoot as well, becoming experts in handling firearms.

The Five Points School, built in 1876, served as a school until 1920.
Since then it has seen many uses. Recently restored, it will become
a meeting hall and the location of an area historical exhibit.

Brick school houses replaced the original frame one-room schools around 1890. This class attended the Keystone school, largest in the township at that time.

The Keystone School was erected in 1896, and used until it was replaced by a new consolidated Chester Center School, built in the center of the township in 1923.

Well drilling and the occasional sight of a gusher characterized life in Chester Township at the end of the 19th century. A few lucky families amassed fortunes from their oil lease revenues.

This store in Keystone (c. 1895) met the area's need for oil well supplies. Well casings were transported on the wagon wheel and axle assemblies (without a wagon bed) that can be seen in front of the store.

Keystone, platted in 1872, prospered for a time by being on the route of the Fort Wayne to Muncie Railroad.

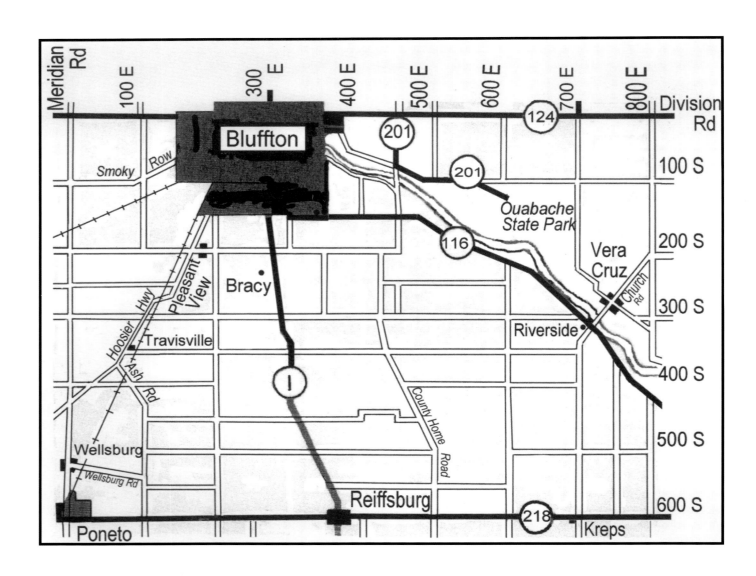

HARRISON TOWNSHIP

4

On June 22, 1837, when the first Wells County commissioners Solomon Johnson, James Scott, and R. C. Bennett held their first meeting, one of their first official actions was to create Harrison and Rockcreek townships. The county was divided into two parts by a line beginning on the southern border of the county and running northward between what is now Chester and Nottingham townships and Liberty and Harrison townships, then two miles east between the present townships of Harrison, and finally north to the county line. The territory east of this line was designated as Harrison Township, and the area west was called Rockcreek Township. By the year 1841 Harrison township was reduced to its present area of forty-eight square miles with an east-west dimension of eight miles and a north-south dimension of six miles.

Early settlers were Charles Bennett and Thomas W. Van Horn in 1834; Gabriel Markley, John Markley, and R. C. Bennett in 1835; Adam Miller, James Guthrie, and Almon Case in 1836; John Burgess, Michael Myers, A. W. Johnson, and Daniel Miller in 1837; M. Michael Whitmer, John Studabaker, Amos Townsend, and C. Chalfant in 1838; Nelson Kellog, William Studabaker, John A. Deam, and William Foncannon in 1839. Almon Case, spent his first three weeks sheltered in a hollow log diagonally across from the present court house, ill with "ague." In the meantime, Adnah Hall, Sr. made his way here in 1837 by swimming swollen streams. Abraham Johnson found his way from Fort Wayne with a compass, and poor Solomon Kemp arrived in 1839 with six motherless children. One of the first physicians was Leonidas Mason, who arrived in 1838, the same year John Studabaker arrived with merchandise and opened a store just north of the present courthouse. A first trustee of Bluffton and later editor of the newspaper, *The People's Press*, came in 1841. These were sturdy souls involved with the history of Bluffton, which was platted in 1838. A more detailed look at the town is considered in another chapter of this book.

EARLY CHURCHES

Six Mile Church, the first organized church in the county, was formed in 1838 by circuit rider Hallet Barber. The congregation first met in the cabin of Thomas and Hannah Van Horn. By 1858 a frame building had been constructed near the Six Mile Creek with a membership of sixty souls. Trustees were Lewis Prillaman, Abram Studabaker, and Jonathon Markley. In 1905, a cement block church was built, but it was destroyed by fire in 1914. The current church was completed in 1915.

Other early churches were the St. John's Reformed Church in Vera Cruz, dedicated in 1854 with a membership of forty, and the Evangelical Association.

Since many of the early residents were of German heritage, it was not surprising that the two early churches in the area were of similar background. Christian Saurer, Peter Meyer, and John Moeschberger were all of the canton of Berne, Switzerland. They were instrumental in obtaining various ministers to preach in their homes. St. John's Reformed Lutheran Church was organized in 1849. A parsonage was built for the minister that also served as a church. In

The Six Mile congregation, organized in 1838, first met in cabins and a log church and then in this building constructed in 1858 on land donated by Adam Miller. The large attendance at this conference indicates the strong influence churches had in the rural community.

1858, a church was dedicated for the Reformed believers. The French who settled in Newville built a small church in 1853 on the northern edge of town. It later became pastorless and finally was used as the parsonage of the brick Reformed Church (constructed in 1897) which was destroyed by fire in recent years. The Rev. Peter Vitz was one of the early ministers and was followed by his sons, Otto Vitz and Oswald P. Vitz, in the pulpit.

The Evangelical Association was organized in 1853 with William Mertz and Jacob Mosiman as members. This church is no longer in existence under that name.

The Apostolic Christian Church, which currently has the largest membership in Wells County, first met in a small log building erected December 24, 1867, near Vera Cruz on the Benedict Baumgartner farm. Mathias Strahm served as the leader of the church, which was once called the Evangelical Baptist. Members came through many miles of mud and bad weather and stayed for an entire day of worship, having lunch at the church. This practice of staying for a light lunch and having an afternoon service exists today. In 1897 a second frame church was built. This was replaced in 1953 with a spacious brick building with a seating capacity of about 1,000 people.

The Bethel Methodist Episcopal Church was dedicated in 1854 with a membership of thirty-five. Even though the congregation is small, it is one of the older church buildings still standing in Harrison township.

TOWNSHIP GROWTH AND DEVELOPMENT

Once the fertile soil of the township was drained with a system of ditches, agriculture became the main source of income for those residing outside Bluffton. The township is bisected by the Wabash River, which is often outside its banks far above flood stage. When this happened in 1875, John Thomas, whose farm lay just south of the Powell Ford in the vicinity of the present White Bridge, was attempting to retrieve shocks of wheat that were floating downstream. He and his son, Adam, were pulling them in as they floated by. However, the prow of the boat met up with a thorn tree, capsizing the canoe and throwing both occupants into the river. Adam grabbed the tree, but Mr. Thomas sank and his body was recovered about a week later at the entrance of the old mill race at the foot of Wabash Street in Bluffton.

Another tragedy occurred years later at the same site, the result of a nitroglycerin explosion. In the 1880s, natural gas was discovered in southern Wells County. The production of nitroglycerin and its delivery to the oil and gas fields were among the companion companies resulting from this oil and gas boom. William Ulmer was killed while crossing the Wabash River at Powell's Ford with a load of nitroglycerin, destroying everything in the vicinity as well as himself, his wagon, and team. The nitroglycerin factory, located on the Byrd farm one mile north of Powell's Ford, also exploded at a later date, killing three.

Much of the history of Harrison Township centers around the city of Bluffton. However, there were some peripheral developments which were noteworthy over the past one hundred and fifty years. During the administration of Franklin D. Roosevelt's New Deal, a CCC (Civilian Conservation Corps) camp was established in Harrison Township along the Wabash River between Vera Cruz and Bluffton. Unemployed young men between the ages of eighteen and twenty-five were housed in the camp and paid $30 per month to do reforestation and construction work in the area. Twenty-two dollars of their pay was sent directly home to their families. Two Bluffton men, Virgil M. Simmons, who was Administrative Officer, Indiana Department of Public Works and Commissioner, Indiana Department of Conservation, and Kenneth M. Kunkel, who was Assistant Commissioner, Indiana Department of Conservation, arranged that the site of the CCC Camp and surrounding acreage was chosen as the site of the Wells County State Forest and Game Preserve. Originally the State Forest was used for wildlife propagation and as a nursery. In more recent years, as a state park, it has developed into a busy tourist attraction for the area, offering spacious camp grounds, fishing and boating, naturalist studies, a modern swimming pool, and other amenities. As such it enriches the income of the entire area.

The County Infirmary was built in 1875 at a cost of $16,000. A new facility was built on the site in 1939 and still stands today, operated by the county as the Maplewood nursing home. The surrounding farm is currently owned by the county.

A two-story brick building, situated three miles south and one-half mile east of Bluffton, was constructed in 1929 at a cost of $25,000 as the Wells County Detention Home. Everett Brown, architect, designed the building, which featured two wings for separation of the sexes. It was built on the site of an old dilapidated building which had been condemned by the state when it refused to give the county a license for its operation. The new structure was designed to house about thirty children, but rarely had more

The White Bridge, so called because the White family owned land near the bridge, was also the early location of Power's Ford, the site of a disastrous nitroglycerine explosion during the oil and gas boom era. The iron bridge was demolished in the 1990s and replaced with a concrete structure.

Civilian Conservation Corps (CCC) workers constructing the service building at the Wells County Game Preserve, known today as Ouabache State Recreation Area.

than twenty occupants. The history behind the construction of the home began in 1923 when citizens first became interested in erecting a new building. According to a newspaper report, the county commissioners, "against their will," were pressured into changing the Wells County Orphanage to the Wells County Detention Home, which placed the home in the control of the circuit judge and the Board of Children's Guardians. After the change, children other than orphans who were classified as wards of the state were admitted. During the years of operation, farming, gardening, and the raising of chickens and cattle were chores for the children at the institution. When the Welfare Department was created in 1936 and assumed control of aid to dependent children and operation of the building, the institution became known as the Children's Home. As the Welfare Department began to place children in private foster homes, fewer children resided in the Children's Home. By January 1949, only one child remained in the home. An inventory taken prior to its closing included 22 iron beds, 314 bales of hay, 112 hens, 22 roosters, three cows, one heifer, and one churn.

TOWNSHIP SCHOOLS

The first school in the county was taught in this township by Jesse B. McGrew in 1837 and was located about two miles north of the courthouse on the farm of Adam Moller. Early frame schools were later replaced by the little one-room brick schoolhouses. Most were heated with a centrally located woodstove and had no lighting, the length of the school day depending upon the amount of daylight. Recesses were spent playing such games as tag, Andy over, black man's bluff, dare base, old witch, and, of course, many games involving a ball. Health standards were never too high. Schools were often closed due to epidemics of flu, smallpox, diphtheria, and tonsillitis. Common remedies were a bag of asafetida tied around the neck, a stink bug tied in a thimble, an onion poultice, or turpentine and lard, all of which served to keep others away if nothing else.

In 1868 a two-story frame school was erected in Vera Cruz that accommodated 125 pupils. The first graded school had two classrooms. Grades one through four were taught downstairs by women teachers, while grades five through eight were taught by men teachers upstairs. The rooms were heated with wood in long iron stoves. An extra vacation day was observed one day when a young gentleman who had just checked his trap line and encountered a skunk while on his way to school, carefully laid his coat near the stove upon entering the classroom.

A new brick building was built in 1896 and had two classrooms and cloak rooms on the top floor. It was heated with a furnace and later remodeled with a dining room and kitchen in the basement. Since there was not much going on in the small town of Vera Cruz, teachers would allow the children to go to the windows to watch a funeral procession passing by on the way to the nearby cemetery.

A lot of attention was paid to penmanship. Longtime teacher Charles Park often required students to write the Star Spangled Banner, the Gettysburg Address, and Old Ironsides from memory, with all the proper punctuation, until a satisfactory style had been achieved. This was Mr. Park's equivalent of today's "time-out" during recess, for students who talked to their classmates or helped them out with their work.

The "Poor Farm School" was so named because it was situated near the County Farm, only a few rods east of the Six Mile Creek on County Farm property. Originally a frame building, it was replaced with a brick school in 1885 or 1886. The children residing in the county orphanage attended this school. One student recalled that, since there was no well, there was always competition to see which two students would carry the three-gallon bucket of water from which all drank, using the same dipper. Ice-skating on Six Mile Creek was the main winter sport for recess and lunchtime. Children took their sleds to school and left them until the spring thaw, taking advantage of the steep slope north of the school.

Smoky Row School allegedly took its name from the continuous line of smoke in the air as forests were cleared and burned for the new Range Line Road, now 600 E. Two frame schools were constructed before the red brick building was built, consisting of one room with a huge stove right in the middle of the floor, its stove pipe fastened by wire attached to the ceiling. A large plus were the two brick outhouses, famous because they were draftless in the winter.

The wildlife exhibit building at the Wells County Game Preserve in the 1940s. The building was demolished when the site became Ouabache State Recreation Area and the wildlife exhibits were eliminated.

Poplar Grove School derived its name from the tall poplar trees on its perimeter. The school year consisted of a four-month winter term and a two-month spring term with a male teacher instructing the winter term and a lady teacher in the spring term when the men were busy in the fields. About 1889, between the winter and spring terms, the little frame school house burned and was replaced with a new brick building. In 1920 a twenty-six room building was constructed, a small portion of which stands today. Other schools included the Section School, the Reiffsburg School, and the Travisville School.

TOWNS AND VILLAGES

As the township became more populated, people began to cluster together in small towns and villages. Mechanicsville, Walmersville, and Winterville were all small and, since they were directly south of Bluffton, became part of that city. It is assumed that the Walmer family and Winter family were the sources for the names of these hamlets. Nothing can be established regarding Pleasant View,

One of the first manual training classes in Wells County schools was at the Poor Farm School in 1907 with Thomas W. Shoup as the teacher.

however there was a regular column appearing in the Bluffton paper reporting the local news (gossip) from Pleasant View. Bracy was the site of storage tanks for pipelines, and over the years it has been the source of one or two serious fires. None of the above villages ever had the prestige of a post office.

REIFFSBURG

Reiffsburg was first called Reiffstown after the man who platted it in 1851, John Reiff. The post office was established September 11, 1854, with Cyrus Van Emon as the postmaster. It was discontinued February 15, 1905. In 1906, Charles Waldo bought the Shoemaker store, only to see it completely destroyed by fire in 1907. In 1908 a new store was opened by Hi Williams and housed in a barn. Business came and left over the years. Today all that remains is a crossroads of two state highways and the Methodist Church, referred to earlier in this chapter.

TRAVISVILLE

Travisville was named for John Travis who laid out the town in 1871. The post office in Travisville was established in 1873 with Charles Cole as the post-master. It was discontinued in January of 1877.

VERA CRUZ AND RIVERSIDE

One of the early larger villages is Verz Cruz, formerly called Newville. The name was changed to Vera Cruz in 1870, as there was another town of Newville in Indiana. It was originally laid out by James Higgins and Christian Sowers in September 1848. Additional early settlers were Peter Meyer and John Moeschberger. Other families coming soon after were the David Buehlers, the William Mertzes, the Jorays, and the Bovines.

The first store was opened by 1859 by Leopold Hirsh and was followed by two other stores in 1860, one started by Anthony Sunier and another by William Mertz. William Mertz, Jr. served as postmaster for thirteen years in this store. Samuel Mosiman also had a hardware store. The first physician, Dr. J. D. Fitzpatrick, arrived in the village the same year. Others were Geisel, Maddox, and McClean.

An early industry was A. Daelhousen's woolen factory, where cloth and yarns were made, beginning in 1875. The factory, operated by steam power, had 180 spindles and one set of cards, and employed five people. The principal product was yarn which was shipped to surrounding towns. A flour mill, originally built on the Wabash River bank in the early years of the village, was remodeled and operated by Isaac North & Company in 1881. It had burrs for both wheat and corn. It was first run by water power and later by a steam engine. Meyer & Gehrig owned a sawmill on the south side of the river, while Ferdinand Biberstein had a sawmill in the town. There was a tile factory and brickyard in the north end of the village. Around the turn of the century an elevator was owned and operated by the Studabaker Grain and Seed Company.

A milk condensing plant, owned by Amos Newhauser, was located on the other side of the river at the crossroads area known as Riverside. Later it was known as the Hoosier Condensary and moved to Bluffton. The Riverside plant closed in 1919 when it was forced to move because the interurban which went from Bluffton to Geneva was no longer operating. R. C. Meyer also owned a general store in Riverside in the 1920-1940 era and operated a "huckster wagon."

Many service facilities existed in Vera Cruz in the later 1800s. M. Hennefort and William F. Mosure were blacksmiths. Samuel Siegrist was the wagon maker. The Jorays were well-diggers, and the town carpenters were the Heche brothers.

Later the Heches operated a grocery store. Fred Beeler sold meat by the front quarter at the price of four cents per pound while the hind quarters cost

Children on their way to school in the Poplar Grove School "Hack" in 1908. This was a typical mode of school transportation used in Wells County during that period.

The Bixler Hotel at Vera Cruz (Newville), the third floor of which was a popular meeting spot for quadrille dancers. Following Bixler's death, this stage coach stop was operated by his wife, a great aunt of Dr. H. D. Brickley of Bluffton.

the grand price of five cents per pound. Due to the German heritage of the area, cheese factories were found all over town, and some even shipped out of state.

The women and children were not forgotten. August Muller and Leonard Tremp were the shoemakers and Mrs. C. Biberstein and Mrs. Waltemath were milliners. Mrs. Maggie Bixler operated the Bixler House, a well-known local hotel which was also a stage coach stop at one time. Ella Batson remembered being taken to the third floor of the hotel to watch the rising Wabash River during the 1913 flood. The dance floor was on the third floor, a popular place for quadrille dancers.

The end of the interurban and development of roads and railroads through Bluffton began the decline of the town. In 1955 the Vera Cruz Opportunity School was started at the site of the original Vera Cruz School, operated by a joint cooperative between Adams and Wells Counties and serving mentally handicapped individuals. It later was also moved to Bluffton and was housed in a new facility. Today there are only three business establishments remaining: the Croy Machine Shop, Rhonda's Clip and Curl, and Camelot, a banquet hall.

—B. Elliott

Albert Selby, George Selby, Cora Selby Hoeppner, Mary Selby, William Selby, and in front, Bessie Selby standing in front of their meat market in 1912.

The Steiner Store, pictured in 1908, was operated at this same location in Vera Cruz until the late 1930s.

The Gottlieb and Magdalena (Minger) Rolli home with the barber shop and Rolli tavern on the right about 1900. The temperance movement resulted in the closing of many taverns in the small towns.

Oris Masterson, Henry Heche, Fred Joray, Fred Wenger, Harold Rolli, and Ed Joray posing in front of Fred Wenger's butcher shop.

A buggy in front of the Cal Rauch home. The Neunschwander Hardware is to the right and St. John's Evangelical and Reformed church is in the background. Cal Rauch had a barber shop in the hardware location in the 1930s and 1940s.

The Case steam engine was used to power the Walter's saw mill in Riverside in 1875. It was also used to power the threshing machine for community threshing rings.

Walter's saw mill lot in Riverside in the 1920s showing the Riverside Condensery (Hoosier Condensery) in the center rear and the Studabaker grain elevator in the right rear. This was located at the southwest corner of present day Indiana 116 and the terminus of Indiana 201.

The Bluffton, Geneva, and Cincinnati Interurban depot at Riverside. The interurban was a transportation boon to the area. The boardwalk on the left led to the Sovine store, later the site of the R. C. Myers general store.

The Riverside Condensery operated by Amos Neuhouser was later moved to Bluffton after the Bluffton-to-Geneva interurban ceased operation.

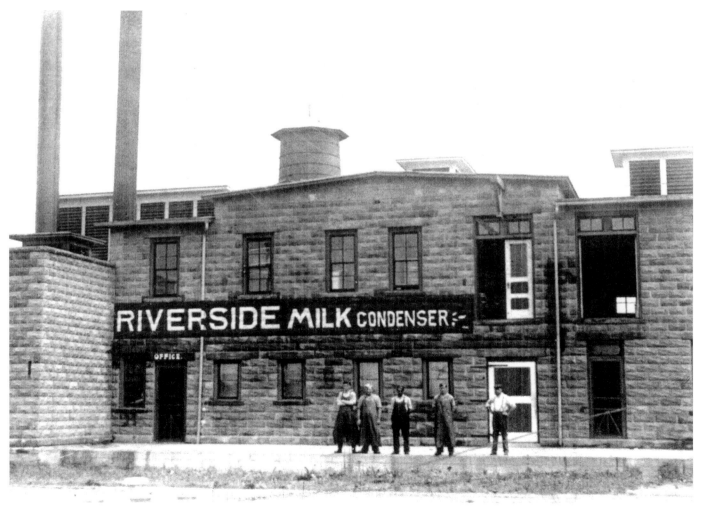

A 1920s scene at Riverside showing the Studabaker Grain and Feed Company, which was located at the southeast corner of the Indiana 201-116 intersection.

After the Riverside Condensery moved to Bluffton, the building was used as a cider mill. Note the mixture of automobiles and buggies at this time.

That same condensery was later used as a shipping point for chickens around 1920.

The R. C. Meyer grocery and residence in 1961 located on the northwest corner in Riverside. For years, Mr. Meyer ran a "huckster wagon" in the area, bringing necessities and food products to the home. The huckster wagon was a general store on wheels and much appreciated by the ladies of the household.

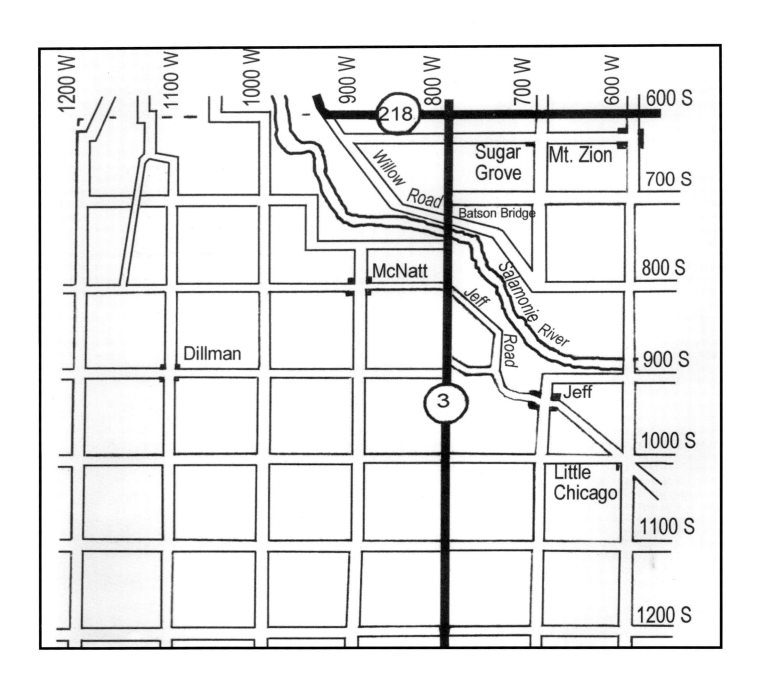

JACKSON TOWNSHIP

5

Jackson Township was set off as a separate unit of government on September 4, 1837. At that time it contained what is now Jackson and Chester townships. Only seven votes were cast in their first election at which a veteran of the War of 1812, Henry McCullick, was elected as trustee. Henry McCullick's oldest son was named justice of the peace, and another son, John, and Lucinda Thompson received the first marriage license on December 7, 1837.

On March 1, 1841, the township was divided when Chester Township was organized. Jackson Township has long been referred to as the "Lost Township" because the surrounding counties of Huntington, Grant, and Blackford were formed so that the area could not be a part of any of the townships without forming a geographical projection. Added to Wells, the county's shape became a reverse "L."

Several speculators purchased land in Wells County when it was first offered for sale by the government, but some never made the arduous journey to visit their property. The first man to buy land in Jackson Township was one of those buying land along the Salamonie River. This area, with its natural drainage and abundance of stone for building purposes, was attractive to those in the east who were able to read the land surveyor's reports, which recorded the soil type, drainage, and forestation.

EARLY SETTLERS

Nathaniel Batson, John Jones, and Daniel Jones, arrived in 1836, locating near the present site of Batson Bridge, across the Salamonie River on what is today State Road 3. Together this group owned more than a thousand acres of land. Many settlers arrived later in 1836 and through 1837 and 1838. Among these entering land on the north side of the river, and with many of their descendants still residing in the township, were Henry Huffman, Phillip Roush, Henry Wolfgang, Sampson Richards, Jacob Clingenpeel, Andrew Morrison, Truman Lounsbury, Chris Miller, George Colbert, and Sam Batson. The central point of this community was the old Batson Cemetery on the north side of the river and east of the Batson bridge.

On the south side of the river were the farms of David Miller, Zebulon Swaim, Henry Wright, Elijah Graves, Jack Perfect, William McIntire, Richard McIntire, James Turner, William Tomlinson, Amos Alspach, Jonathan

Henry Huffman built this cabin in 1837 for his family two and a quarter miles west of Mt. Zion. The ends of poles can be seen which support a loft for the bedrooms.

Progress allowed Henry Huffman to replace his 1837 cabin with a new home of frame construction. Levi and Martha Huffman are in the picture with Henry.

With only candles for light, tin lanterns, with holes and slits were used to safely hold a candle while being carried about.

Lee, Bowen Thorp, Robert Alexander, William Rea Sr., John McFadden, Reason Bevington, Burket Elkins, Samuel Palmer, John Bocher Sr., John Baker Sr., William Burkland, and Joel Ebersole.

PIONEER LIFE

Jacob Minnich came to the township in 1836, entering his land about one-half mile north of the Batson Bridge. After constructing a rude cabin, he returned east, bringing his family to their new home the following fall. Minnich became ill with ague (malaria) upon their arrival, unable to construct a barn shelter for his horses. The horses had to be left outside for the winter, tied to the wagon that brought the family and their belongings to Indiana. After Jacob's recovery in the spring, he was able to build a log stable. During that summer, he took part in twenty-one log rollings and cabin raisings in the neighborhood. His seven year old son, John, learned to drive the horses that summer; in the fall of 1836 he drove the team to take their first crop of corn to Huntington, a trip that took more than three days. Some of the corn was traded for salt, which sold for ten to thirteen dollars a barrel. This price remained constant until the completion of the canal to Huntington when the lower cost of transportation lowered the cost of the many eastern products the settlers needed but couldn't provide from their land.

Many sugar-maple trees were growing on the Minnich farm, and one season when sugar was very valuable, 2200 pounds of maple sugar were boiled down from the sap. It was on this farm and from these sugar trees that the Sugar Grove Church took its name.

Oliver Jones, arriving in 1845, felled trees on his farm, and fastening the logs together, rafted them down the Salamonie River to the saw mill at Warren. Here they were sawed into lumber. This was the first lumber used to build a frame house in the township.

The life of these early settlers was harsh and isolated but they were able to bring fun and sociability into it. "Bees" were a way to socialize and were held for any reason as a way to get together. If there was a house, a barn, or a church to build, quilting to be done, corn husking, spinning, or weaving—then a "bee" would be organized with "many hands to make work light." And after the work was done, a time of fun began with feasting, dancing, and singing.

SUGAR GROVE CHURCH

Until school houses were built, where church services were held in the early days, frequent community church services were held in the Jacob Minnich home. A German Baptist Church was built on the west side of the road, just north of the Batson Bridge. After the frame was constructed, there was a conflict in the plans and the building was abandoned. (A few years later the site was taken over and completed by the New Light Christian Church.) A second attempt to build a Baptist church was made. This building was constructed on the Minnich farm and became known as the Sugar Grove Church. This church played an important role in the life of the community for over a half century, being used until 1930. The building was later sold, moved to a farm three-fourths of a mile west of McNatt and used as a barn.

SCHOOLS

The first school in Jackson Township was a log structure built in 1840, just north of Batson Bridge, on the east side of State Road 3. Pupils were seated on benches made of logs, hewn smooth, and with four legs inserted in holes bored at an angle. Windows were covered with greased paper. John Minnich, who attended the school, later in his life told the story that during the winter months, when snowballs flew through the air, thick and fast, one occasionally penetrated a window. Punishment for the deed usually consisted of replacing the window covering. Paper was so scarce that this meant going to the home of one or two settlers known to have newspapers, securing one, having it greased, and putting it into place.

To keep the school room warm, logs felled in the surrounding forest by the larger pupils were burned in the huge fireplace. The fireplace was constructed of "jambs" faced with clay, on which the flue was built. The flue was built of riven slats covered and laid in clay mortar. The same clay mortar was plastered all over the inside of the fireplace and flue. This clay covering helped prevent the wood from igniting, but with a fire too hot, even the clay covering could not prevent a fire. Many log structures caught fire and burned when a fireplace fire was unattended and got out of control.

This school was attended by pupils from several miles around. With no tax levy then to support the school, each patron contributed toward its support

Log cabins continued to provide housing throughout Wells County into the late 1800s. The family and their cabin were pictured in Jackson Township in 1865. Frame and masonry construction gradually replaced the log homes. Only a few remained by the end of the 19th century, and of those, many were used as utility buildings after the family moved into a modern home which gave them better protection from the elements, but were still without indoor plumbing and electricity.

according to the number of children that he had enrolled. The teacher's salary was usually stated in terms of board and room, plus an amount of money for the year's term. The teacher "boarded around" with the families represented in the school, the stay with each family depending upon the number of pupils from the family attending the school.

The township attracted settlers rapidly after 1840. Other schools were built, most being two miles apart except where the Salamonie River caused an irregular arrangement. These log structures were soon replaced with frame buildings of a more modern type. In turn they were gradually replaced by one-room brick buildings. There were ten one-room schools, each served by a faithful teacher, who had to divide his/her time with all grade levels, first to eighth. In 1917, School District Number 1 had the most modern one-room school in Wells County. It had a complete basement with a furnace, a water pressure system, and flush toilets. Several other districts by

The Asbury Chapel Methodist Church was organized in 1838 but disbanded in 1872. During the 1890s oil boom, the church was reorganized and this church was built next to the Asbury Chapel Cemetery at 1100 South on State Road 3.

1920 gained new modern buildings replacing older buildings destroyed by a wind storm. By 1935, only a few of these brick buildings were in use—the others had deteriorated beyond repair. High school students were being sent into other townships. Lee Morrison, township trustee, began construction of a large grade and high school at Jackson Center, using bricks from the old buildings. Built in 1938, it was used until the 1970s.

The first teacher in the township was reported to be Sampson Richards. William and Hobert Alexander and James Wright were among those who taught in the first log school houses north of Batson bridge.

BRIDGE HISTORY

Bridges were important for the settlers who needed to cross the Salamonie River, which separated the northeastern section of the township. Two bridges constructed of hewn logs spanned the river. One was west of the Batson Cemetery in section 11, the other was located farther south. These two bridges were replaced by a covered bridge, known as the Batson Bridge. Because of difficulties with ice and flood, construction of the covered bridge took nearly three years. The Batson covered bridge stood until 1910 when a new concrete bridge was begun. This bridge, on State Road 3, was replaced in 1934 by the state. In 1882, the Twin Bridges were built near the Chester-Jackson township line.

LOST LAKES

In 1900, Jackson Township completed the graveling of all roads except a section through the "Lost Lakes," a marshy area one mile east of the center of the township. Early settlers reported two lakes, one of eighty acres and another of forty acres. The name "Lost Lakes" had been given because of being in the "lost" township. Others referred to them as the "twin lakes." In 1921, a ditch was constructed to drain the lakes. This lowered the water level four feet, and in subsequent years, the lakes have become no more than ponds.

Land surrounding these ponds is very marshy—animals, straying too near the water's edge have been known to sink beneath the mud and muck. A road was

originally built around the east edge of the lakes, but it was thought that a road could be built across the ridge between the two lakes. Trees were laid with thousands of loads of dirt dumped on top. The fill sank down to the water level. The road was only usable during dry seasons. In 1916, another attempt was made to build a grade for the road, but this again settled to the water level.

The prospect of having a state road through the region in 1930 caused the township to try once more to build a road that the state would accept. Finally the state took it over. Ten acres of soil, six feet deep were placed on the road bed, making a grade about eight feet above the water level. This, too, began to gradually settle. The state decided to blacktop the section, instead of using concrete as had been done on the rest of the road. After many years, the road bed has stabilized.

BLACK GOLD

The oil fever of the 1890s included Jackson Township. A 1962 Indiana Department of Conservation Geologic Survey map shows the location of at least sixty-four wells driven in many of the townships sections. Oil leases contributed to the wealth of many landowners. The crude oil pumped from the Wells County wells contained sulfur compounds, not easily removed at that time, reducing its value after later discoveries in Illinois and Kansas. The lack of a railroad within the township diverted most of the business activity to the surrounding area.

JACKSON TOWNS

Jackson Township claims only six towns and villages in its history whose locations have been recorded on maps: McNatt, Dillman, Jeff, Sugar Grove, Little

Education was a priority throughout Wells County. Schooling first took place in the homes, and as more families arrived, schoolhouses were built of logs with a fireplace for heat. The older boys in the class cut wood for the fire and kept it going. If the wood in the clay covered fireplace caught fire, they were responsible for dousing the flames with water, or snow if available.

Chicago, and Batson Bridge. It does share Mt. Zion with Chester Township, with Mt. Zion on the county line between the two townships. McNatt, Dillman, and Jeff had streets lined with stores and taverns to meet the needs of the oil workers during the 1890–1900 period. The oil field activity could be judged by the number of saloons in the nearby towns.

McNatt, once a flourishing country town with a post office, was named by its founder, George McNatt, who opened and operated the town's grocery and hardware store. Later the store continued in business under the ownership of Jack Monce and his wife Mary Ann. Jack began working in the store for his uncle when he was twelve years old. At that time it was still in the original building, which Jack Monce said "dates back 150 years." When Jack began his career, the store operated a huckster wagon, bringing the store's merchandise to the outlying farms for selection and barter. People then traded their eggs and produce for groceries.

This two-room brick schoolhouse was built at Dillman in 1898.

Today, a visit to the old time general store is like a visit to the past, with the inventory of the material things of today's economy set in yesterday's environment.

Andrew Dillman, a Kentuckian by birth, came to Wells County with his thirteen children and settled in section 19. Later his son, Sidney, started a blacksmith shop on the farm, adding hardware. A store was built nearby, operated by Henry Templeton.

When a post office was located here, the town became known as Dillman, named after Andrew Dillman. Its 1895 population enumerated twenty-eight persons.

Jackson Township shared the oil boom of the 1890s until about 1910 with Nottingham and Chester Townships. The population of 1,700 in 1890 rose to 2,200 in 1900. But by 1910 the population dropped back to 1,700 as the oil and gas wells were depleted and people who had entered the area in pursuit of the oil and gas moved their drilling equipment to newly discovered fields in southern Illinois and Missouri to again seek their fortunes. The remaining population could not support the once bustling activity the towns and their storekeepers had enjoyed.

Today, only the names of some of the towns of Jackson Township remain on maps. Their once important part in the life of the community has been blurred by the advances of the century, but their place in the growth and development of Wells County will not be forgotten.

—*P. Bender*

Jackson Township's consolidated school was built in 1938 with plans from the Everett I. Brown architectural firm in Indianapolis. Brown was a native of Bluffton and designed many Wells County School buildings. The school, located at the northwest corner of section 16, was abandoned in the 1970s with the development of the Southern Wells School system.

The type of drilling "rig" used in southern Wells County in the 1890-1910 oil boom days. The derrick was erected to hold the well casing that was lowered as drilling of the "hole" progressed. The wells were drilled to a depth of more than 1,000 feet, with varying degrees of success. Some turned out to be "dry holes."

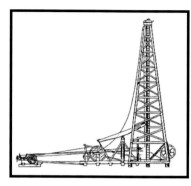

The Robert A. Kilander home on 600 West, near 1100 South in Jackson Township is an example of the wealth that a few lucky families derived from the oil boom. Built in 1900 at a cost of $8000, it was designed by Bluffton architect Cuno Kibele in the colonial revival style. At that time it was reported to be the finest home in the county. Kilander had dried all of the various lumber species used in its construction for twelve years.

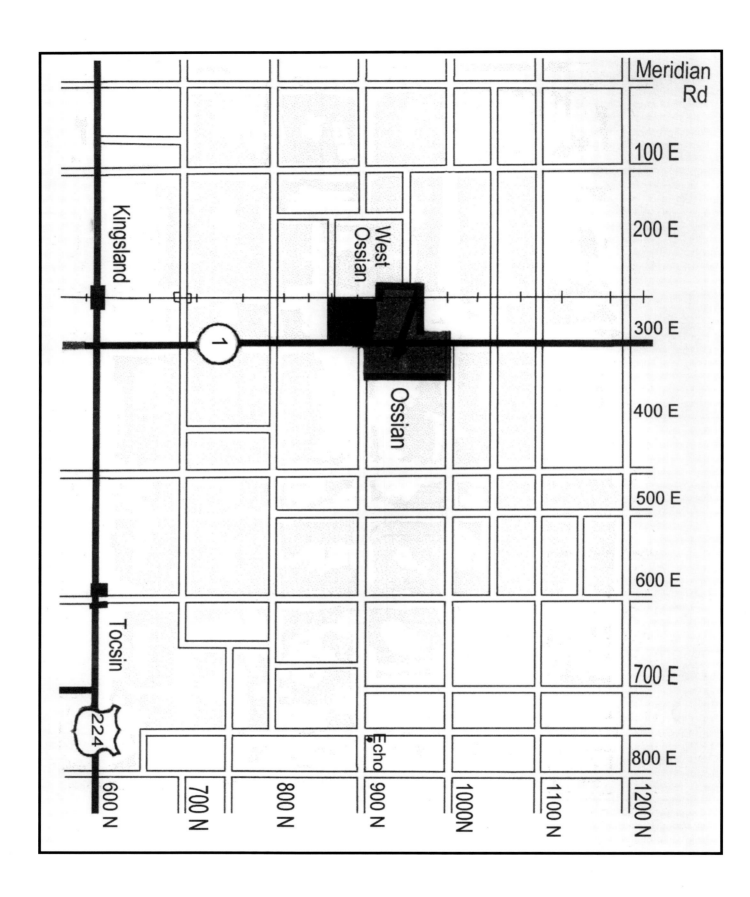

JEFFERSON TOWNSHIP

6

At the time of the organization of Wells County, February 2, 1837, the area now known as Jefferson Township was included in Harrison Township. Jefferson township was organized on the petition of William Craig and Samuel Weston, and by order of the county commissioners.

The first settlers were Samuel Ogden and Robert and William Craig in 1837; Richard Treenary, Thomas and James Furgason, Robert Elwell, and Adam Hatfield in 1838; John Davis, Jacob Bunn, Levi Young, Robert Ewell, Phillip Sower, Samuel Weston, and John Snider in 1839; J. R. LaFever, John Ritter, Jacob and Martin King, William Webster, and John Ogden in 1840. Joseph Gorrell arrived in 1845.

The first township election was held at the home of William Craig on April 6, 1840. Samuel Ogden was the inspector. The new officers were: Phil Sower, Richard Treenary, and Adam Hatfield, trustees; George Weston, clerk; Jacob Bunn, treasurer; John Ritter and John Snyder, overseers of the poor; Jacob King and William Craig, fence viewers; Samuel Weston, justice of the peace; and Jacob Bunn, constable.

The first merchant in the township was John T. Glass in 1840. He bought and sold livestock. In 1843 a dirt road ran from Fort Wayne to Bluffton, but traveling over it was very slow and dangerous. In 1851 a plank toll road was built. Any horseman or driver of a horse-drawn vehicle had to pay a toll. An old story handed down through the years tells of a horse that had become stuck in the mud and only his head was showing. In 1851, Gibson Wilson was named the first road supervisor.

The new trustees met June 1, 1840, and divided the township into three road districts. Samuel Ogden, Samuel Weston, and Thomas Furgason were appointed supervisors. The first road east was Furgason Road (now Davis Road), while the first road west was Mill Street.

In 1854, Captain Karns built a bridge over Eight-Mile Creek, which had earlier been called Bee Creek. The township is drained by Eight-Mile Creek, which runs through the area in a northwest direction. Along the upper part of the stream were extensive marshes, which eventually were properly drained and made them the most productive lands in the township.

On March 14, 1850, the town of Ossian was laid out by William Craig, John Ogden, and Squire LeFever. They sold the town in lots. Ossian's first post office was called Bee Creek, and was started in May of 1850. Levi Young was postmaster. On November 16, 1854, the Ossian post office was established with John Cartwright as the postmaster. In 1852 William Clark came to this township. He was a farmer and mechanic, and also manufactured saddletrees.

In 1886 businesses in or around Ossian were: the hotel "Ossian House," general stores, drug stores, a millinery, a grocery, a blacksmith shop, William Earl's wagon shop, tin shops, shoe shops, a harness shop, meat market, barrel stave factory, a grist mill, a cheese factory, and the Rankin Tannery.

The first school trustees were Levi Young, J. R. Lefever, and John Ogden. They were elected on August 8, 1841, at the home of William Craig. The township was then formed into one school district. The first school was called Craig

Eight-mile creek looking south from Mill Street Bridge.

School, and the first teacher was Miss Margaret Hatfield. This school was a log building. Books were scarce and goose quills were used for pens. Other early teachers were: Isaac Hatfield, Joseph Lefever, and Doctor William Johnston.

The first school in Ossian was taught by Robert M. Johnston. It was organized in 1850. In 1861 a new schoolhouse was built. It was a small log building. Miss Mary Cartwright was the teacher. Other early teachers were: Jacob J. Todd, Maggie Hawkins, and A. B. Cartwright. In the late 1860s a new frame, two-story school was built while Dr. J. I. Metts was trustee. He served twenty-one years in that capacity. The first teacher in this new school was Miss Jennie Sterling.

Other early township schools were: Beck, Caston, Milliken, Bethel, Glass, Bunn, Jackson (Echo), Tocsin, Beatty, Greenwood, Frogpond, and Bethlehem.

When the Civil War started in 1861, Lincoln called for 75,000 volunteers to serve the Union, 12,000 of which were to come from Indiana. Indiana ranked second in the nation for number of volunteers. The attack on Fort Sumter brought out the greatest number of volunteers.

Those in Jefferson Township of Wells County hoped that in fighting on the Union side they would defend and maintain supremacy of the Constitution, and as soon as these objectives were met, the war would be over.

The day following the attack of Fort Sumter, in April of 1861, sixteen Wells County men enlisted. Uriah Todd was the first to enlist. A fund totaling $83,000 was pledged for bounties and relief for soldier's families.

The G. A. R. Post #169 met for many years dedicated to the memory of the Jefferson Township men who contributed their courage and faith to the Union cause. This post was named in memory of Lieutenant-Colonel William Swaim, who, when the Civil War began, raised Company A from Ossian, Murray, and Bluffton volunteers. He was soon elected captain of Company A when the 34th regiment was organized. Swaim was killed in the battle of Champion Hills. He is buried in the Oak Lawn Cemetery, where his regiment officers erected a monument in his memory. He was the father of David H. Swaim, publisher of the Bluffton *News-Banner*.

Following the Civil War, commercial life became very active in Indiana with an era of growth and prosperity setting in. New industry and manufacturing started, and towns which had been little more than crossroads became thriving villages overnight. Villages became active corporations with plans to pave their streets, provide lighting for their businesses and residents, and erect public buildings.

Between 1865–1873, money was plentiful, but soon the inevitable happened. In 1873, a great financial panic swept the country. Factories closed, banks failed, railroad building stopped, money became scarce, and many were unemployed. Gradually business revived and the state turned to developing her natural resources and establishing more manufacturing and commercial interests. Corn and wheat were Indiana's main products. Other industries were coal mining and building stone quarrying.

The township grew rapidly and by 1880 the township had 2,262 residents. In 1882 the first telephones were brought to the Ossian area by the Bell Company.

In 1883 Mark Gorrell had a job as the telegraph operator. Abner Elzey started the first funeral parlor in 1893. Jefferson township resident John Stine served as Wells County recorder from 1895 to 1898.

The township had many early churches. Bethel United Bretheren Church was dedicated in August of 1872. The Presbyterian Church was organized on June 10, 1840, at the home of Adam Hatfield. The Reverend Isaac A. Ogden led the meeting. The first church building was built in 1858 while the Reverend W. Donaldson was pastor. The Methodist Episcopal Church was built in 1866. The Christian Church was organized on November 20, 1872, and their church was dedicated November 3, 1873. The Salem Methodist Episcopal Church was built in 1876. The Zion United Bretheren Church was a log building originally built by the Methodists. It was later purchased for the United Bretheren Congregation

Jefferson Township—District #4 (Bethel School) was built in 1897, Ransom Allen was a trustee.

Lt. Col. William Swaim is buried in the Oak Lawn Cemetery in Ossian. His regiment officers erected a monument in his memory.

by H. S. Davidson, Peter Moneysmith, and James Shuey. The Olive Branch Baptist Church was built in 1869 with land donated by John Caston, who also owned a sawmill in this township. The Elhanan Presbyterian Church was built in 1845 on land donated by Robert Elwell.

ECHO

W. H. Rupright laid out the village of Echo in 1878. Echo was at the crossroads of 1000 North and 750 East. In the 1920s, a tile mill and sawmill were located there. It was recorded that a tornado went through Echo in 1920. Dan Hoover ran a store in the village, and Peter and Sophia Yager lived nearby.

GREENWOOD

Greenwood was named for Samuel Greenwood. The town was platted by Thorton Hunter, John Woodwood, and James Chalfant on September 4, 1871. The town was located one-fourth mile west of State Road One on 700 North.

The Ogden and Chalfant sawmill was destroyed by fire. Around 1884, Greenwood had an organization called the "Jolly Club." Early settlers were the George Nevius family, the Osborns, and the Cartwrights.

The Greenwood School still stands on the southwest corner of State Road One and 700 North, although today it is a family residence. One of the early teachers there was Elizabeth Chalfant Fryback. Besides its use as a school, the building was used for Grange meetings, box socials, and spelling bees.

KINGSLAND

Kingsland is three and one-half miles south of Ossian and six and one-half miles north of Bluffton, on the dividing line between Jefferson and Lancaster townships.

The first post office was established as Parkinson on June 9, 1882. The town was laid out in June 11, 1883, and was originally called Parkinson. It was named in honor of their first postmaster and prominent citizen, Ebenezer Parkinson. In 1883 William Parkinson made tile here, a Mr. Brunson ran a drygoods store, and a Mr. Stoller ran a grocery.

The town was later renamed Kingsland by Isaac Hatfield on April 21,1884. While history does not reveal any verifiable facts, old settlers say the name of Kingsland was chosen because land in the vicinity was very productive. The name showed a desire to indicate the land was "fit for a king." Kingsland was a station on the east-west Chicago-Erie Railroad and later on the north-south Fort Wayne, Bluffton, Muncie, and Indiana Traction line.

Early settlers in and around Kingsland included Daniel K. Hanna, Wilson Donaldson, David T. Wasson, and Evan L. Chalfant. There was a Methodist Church here at one time. The Presbyterian Church was organized in 1886 and a church building was dedicated in the spring of 1887.

In 1889 the Kingsland area had a diphtheria epidemic. It was at this time that the county organized a Board of Health. E. C. Vaughn served as the board's first president.

The Kingsland Hotel was built in 1891, and can still be seen on the southwest corner of the intersection of Highway 1 and U. S. 224. It is now a private residence.

It was reported that an exploratory well came in nicely with both oil and gas present in March of 1892, but nothing further came of it and the expected oil field did not materialize. Many in the area were sorely disappointed.

In 1912 John Abram operated a blacksmith shop at Kingland. At Kingsland Corners, the Tower Service Station was operated by Roscoe Woodward from 1927 until 1968. Other businesses were Hoovers Grocery (they also had a huckster wagon); Ira Hoover, barber; and the Kahn family scrap and junkyard, which they ran for many years. Russell Somers worked at the Erie Railroad Depot for many years.

On September 21, 1910, a gruesome interurban wreck occurred near Kingsland. It was the most deadly event to have taken place in Wells County. Forty-two of the forty-six passengers and crew aboard perished in the accident. Most of the passengers were enroute to the Allen County Fair in Fort Wayne when their northbound car smashed into a empty southbound car that was on its way to Bluffton to handle the increased traffic caused by the fair. Of the death toll, twenty-five were residents of Wells County, which put the entire county into shock. The blame for not clearing the tracks for a regularly scheduled run has never been completely placed, but further disaster was averted when a car following a short distance behind was flagged to a stop, thus avoiding a larger pile-up.

One reason for the severity of the accident was the higher-built construction of the southbound car that telescoped into the lower, lighter northbound car. If a passenger survived the impact without a broken neck, then the onslaught of the floor of the heavier car caught him momentarily. The few survivors were either thrown clear or had their necks protected.

Greenwood School was built around 1883. Today it is a private residence, at the corner of State Road One and 700 North.

Older citizens of the county carry vivid memories of the tragedy. Most were acquainted at least indirectly with some victim. There was a temporary morgue set up in an empty store building in Bluffton. Schools were closed for one week in mourning for the victims.

WEST OSSIAN

West Ossian was laid out on October 8, 1870, and platted by J. N. Glass, T. B. Hunter, John Glass, William B. Miller, G. W. Glass, George Harter, Adam Hatfield, W. S. Mannes, and James Gorrell. Other early pioneers were Joseph Elzey and the Reverend Wilson Donaldson. Ossian and West Ossian were initially separated by the marshes along Eight-Mile Creek.

Frank Hendry bought one-half interest in the Rex and Hendry Tile Factory in 1899. Also located in West Ossian, a stave and heading factory was owned and operated by the Caston family.

There was a Parkinson Grocery in West Ossian; H. C. Parkinson ran a huck-

In the foreground is a waiting room as provided by the interurban at crossroads stops. The traction line crossed the Erie Railroad at Kingsland.

ster wagon from there. Other businesses in the area were the stockyards; Doan and Beaty Lumber Company; Burnett and Timbrook, grain elevator; John Goshosn's store (which sold hardware and implements for Shephard and Goshorn); and John Hanna, harness maker.

David Lautzenheiser and Ward Brickley were telegraph operators for the Erie Railroad. Joseph Brown ran a livery and feed barn, and Matthew Burnett was postmaster. Clarence Birkfield was an agent for the Wells Fargo Company. Sam and Martin Sturgeon were also well-known citizens living near West Ossian.

David Craig brought honor to this township when he drove the third spike used on the lines of the first Wells County railroad. The railroad had been surveyed as early as 1854, but rails were not laid though West Ossian until 1869, due to the scarcity of capital during the Civil War period.

The interurban ran through West Ossian in 1905. In 1912 Nelson Biddle was section foreman and John Branagan was roadmaster for the L. E. and W. Railroad.

In 1929 the Ku Klux Klan, which from time to time emerges from the shadows to preach its doctrine of hatred, burned a cross in West Ossian, causing a great uproar for a time.

TOCSIN

This small village is located nine miles north of Bluffton and three miles east of State Road One on U.S. 224.

The definition of the word tocsin is: "An alarm sounded on a bell." It is believed that warning bells that were used on the older steam locomotives on the railroad may be how Tocsin got its name. Switch engines would use their bells to warn residents at railroad crossings.

Early settlers to this area were Michael Blue, Samuel Kunkel, Ivan Richey, and the Kleinknight family.

Michael Blue was born April 16, 1836, in Miami County, Ohio. His family moved to Wells County-Section 15 in Lancaster Township when he was four years old. Mr. Blue was the Wells County surveyor from 1868-1871 and auditor from 1872-1875. He also served as a county commissioner. On April 28, 1883, he platted the town of Tocsin. He also spent time as a state legislator. His son, Capolis L. Blue was a doctor and surgeon in the Tocsin area.

When Mr. Blue heard of the railroad coming to this area, he wrote his brother-in-law, Samuel Kunkel, who at the time resided in Missouri. He told him that this might be a good opportunity to open a new store.

Samuel Kunkel bought the original forty-acre tract upon which Mr. Blue laid out the town. Kunkel's first addition was platted August 19, 1884, and the second Kunkel addition on November 18, 1884. Mr. Kunkel was the first postmaster and served in that capacity until 1887. He also ran a hotel and opened the first grain business in town. His daughter Iva was the first white child born in Tocsin. She later married Bill Jones, whose main occupation was buying chickens.

Wesley Sowards built the first residence in town. Dr. Noah Bergman was the first doctor.

This area was relatively low in elevation, and to the east and west it was lower still. There were muck areas in both directions, which would frequently catch fire and burn for long periods of time. Flooding was also a serious problem in the area, and it was a long time before adequate drainage was provided. For years, all the roads were dirt, and in the spring they turned to mud. There were times when the horses could not pull even empty wagons. Some farmers had lightweight wagon boxes with narrow wheels. These were referred to as "Chinese Cutters," and were sometimes used in bad weather.

The road that is now U.S. 224 was known as the Harding Highway, named after Warren G. Harding, who was president of the United States from 1921-1923. It was so designated by Rand & McNally, the mapmakers, and was marked by a big "H" painted on the telephone poles by the roadside. It was part of a coast-to-coast highway and was very heavily traveled even before it was paved.

A brick street was built in 1926. There was no electricity in Tocsin until 1928.

Kingsland Hotel was built in 1910. The hotel was moved to the corner of U.S. 224 and State Road 1. Today it is a private home.

Roscoe and Lela Woodward owned and operated the Tower Service Station at the corner of State Road 1 and U.S. 224. The station closed during the 1960s.

The railroad was built through this area in 1882. It was first known as the Chicago & Atlantic Railroad. Later it became known as the Chicago & Erie Railroad, but named after Erie, Pennsylvania. After World War II it was known as the Erie-Lackawana. The Erie was one of the largest haulers of freight in the world. At one time there were three passenger trains a day to serve the people of the community. One of the passenger trains was nicknamed "the Dummy." Hugh Dailey and George Rupright were engineers on the Erie and would signal to the people each time they came through. You could send telegrams from the railroad depot. Merchandise, lumber, supplies, and large mail order items arrived daily. The first depot agent is not known, but Wilson Kreigh was full-time agent for many years.

Tocsin was a thriving little community and in 1887 the population was 150 residents. In 1899 the Knights of the Pythias lodge was founded in town. The Pythian Sisters was organized and chartered in 1906. There was also a Modern Woodman lodge in Tocsin at one time.

The Bank of Tocsin organized in 1912 with Thomas J. Sowards, president; G. W. Rupright, vice-president; and Frank Garton, cashier. The bank closed in 1925, and this had a devastating effect on the entire community.

James Coffield and Jonathan Myers were blacksmiths in 1912. John O. Dailey operated the stockyards. In 1916, John Carl Gallivan moved to Tocsin and joined in partnership with Mr. Dailey, and the firm became Dailey, Gallivan, and Rupright. Receiving stations for livestock were at Preble, Craigville, Uniondale, and Tocsin. Livestock was shipped by rail to Chicago, Buffalo, Indianapolis, and Cincinnati.

Tocsin built a new school 1908. Its cornerstone tells us it was built during the years that Arthur R. Huyette was Wells County's school superintendent. For many years Tocsin did have a high school along with a grade school. Several years later the high school grades were discontinued, but the grade school operated until the spring of 1941. The school was then closed and the students were transferred to Ossian. The school's last principal was Miles Hoopengardner.

Through the years Tocsin has had many businesses, the Hall and Garton Store, the Hartman and Cash hardware store, three saloons, a stove factory, a hoop factory, and a brick factory. Amos and Harry Byrd ran a tile factory near Tocsin. There were also several general stores, barber shops, a hardware store, a harness shop, a drugstore, a butcher shop, a poultry house, a carriage shop, and several restaurants.

After Arthur P. Kelley quit working for the railroad he ran a drugstore and a lumberyard. He also took delivery of the first gasoline-powered automobile in Tocsin. In 1908 he established the first service station in town.

At one time Tocsin had a small orchestra. William Teunison was manager of the Tocsin Telephone Company. Wilson Kreigh ran the Wells Fargo Company and Express.

—L. Sawyer

The Wabash Valley Interurban wreck happened near Kingsland, Indiana, on September 21, 1910. Forty-one people were killed.

E. T. HAWLEY...

Contractor
and Builder.

Always Up-To-Date
in interior and
Exterior Designing.

Estimates Furnished
upon Application.

NOTE. In the foregoing pages of this edition appear views of residences designed and constructed or remodeled under my direction. Mrs. Wm. Lopshire, T. A. Doan, Dr. M. N Newman, W. R. Beaty, J. H. Young, J. H. Keefer, Dr. A. H. Metts, Dr. A. G. Gorrell, Harry Bunn, James Swaim.

TILE ALL SIZES.

Latest Improved Machinery and Dry Kiln.
Estimates gladly furnished on large orders.

PRICES REASONABLE.

Hydralic Cider Press...

All the conveniences for cider making in season.

REX & HENDRY. OSSIAN, IND.
Yards ¼ mile south of Depot.

Rex & Hendry Tile Mill Ad

WM. R. BEATY.   THOS. A. DOAN.

Established 1875

BEATY & DOAN

DEALERS IN

LUMBER
LATH
SHINGLES
AND MOULDING.

Manufacturers
of BRICK

BUYERS and SHIPPERS of

ALL KINDS
OF GRAIN...

BEATY & DOAN,
OSSIAN, INDIANA.

LOCAL AND LONG DISTANCE TELEPHONE NO. 7.

Mill, Elevator and Brick Yard in West Ossian.

Beaty & Doan Tile Mill Ad

Ossian Railroad Depot

**Early plat map of Ossian
and West Ossian**

Levy Grain Company

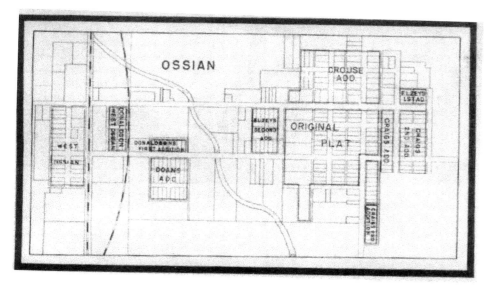

Ben Levy Grain Co.

OSSIAN, INDIANA

Grain-Feeds-Seeds-Coal

———

GRINDING A SPECIALTY
MASTER MIX FEEDS

———

WE BUY AND SELL FARM SEEDS

The Bank of Tocsin was organized in 1912. The bank closed after many years of fine service in 1925.

Tocsin School was built in 1908.

The Wassons General Store

WASSON'S
General Store
GROCERIES
MEATS
LUNCH
HD'W.

PHONE
1 on 27
Tocsin

Top photo: Notice the gas pump in front of this Tocsin store.

Hall and Garton Store

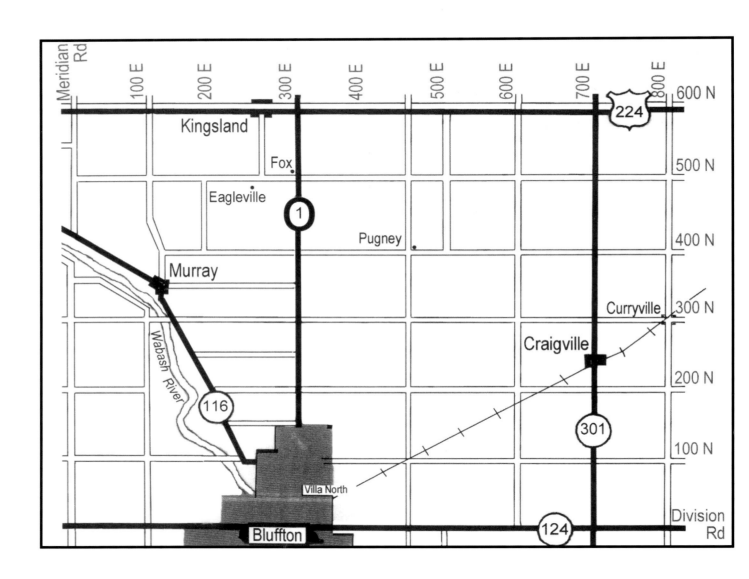

LANCASTER TOWNSHIP

7

Lancaster Township came into existence on March 1, 1841, by taking a six-mile square from what had been Harrison Township on the east and combining it with a two-by-six mile area that was formerly part of Rockcreek Township. Lancaster Township has the distinction of being the location of the very earliest settlements in Wells County. Dr. Joseph Knox settled near the village of Lancaster in 1829, the first white man to establish a home in the county. His cabin was the first settlement between Fort Recovery, Ohio, and Huntington, Indiana. Soon he was joined by his two sons-in-law, Vertress and Warner. He and several of his neighboring settlers fled the county because of the unrest of the Indians that culminated in the Black Hawk War. Their departure left only the families of Henry and Jacob Miller in the county. Henry Miller, a native of Tennessee, had settled on the Knox clearing. Isaac and Allen Norcross arrived in 1831, and left when the Indian problem arose, although Isaac returned later. Robert Harvey returned after the Indian threat no longer existed and settled on land near Murray. The patent for this land was signed by President Andrew Jackson on September 2, 1831.

James Harvey, a brother of Robert, settled in the autumn of 1833. It was in his crude log cabin, without doors or windows and using blankets to keep out the cold, that the first wedding in the area took place. It was the marriage of Rebecca Davis and Robert Simison.

At the Old Settler's celebration on July 4, 1859, Henry Miller described the lifestyle that prevailed when he arrived in the fall of 1832. "When I first arrived here, I had to get wheat from the Godfrey farm on the Salamonie, haul it to Fort Wayne to get it made into flour for my family, and then home again, making a distance of over 100 miles. There was no road part of the way, except as I cut it, and the other part over roads with the solid bottom under thick mud. When I couldn't get to the mill, we had to eat green corn and potatoes if we had them. If not, we managed to get along on dried venison and other wild meat."

A historical marker, west of the present Murray bridge over the Wabash River, notes the site of the birth of the first white child in Wells county, Elizabeth Miller—the daughter of Mr. and Mrs. Henry Miller. She married Jacob Harvey, son of Robert Harvey. After the organization of Wells County other early settlers were Jacob Miller, Thomas Wilkins, and W. P. and Lucinda Davis in 1837; Uriah Blue in 1839; and George and Sarah Wasson in 1841.

Early settlers toiled diligently clearing the dense forests and draining the swamps. One of the large swamps was located near Murray and known as Bear Swamp. The pioneers lived in lean-to cabins surrounded by forests full of ferocious animals and always in danger from unfriendly Indians. Bowen Hale, the first store keeper, traded brass rings, whiskey, and clothing to the Indians for pelts, and then sent Henry Miller to Dayton, Ohio to trade the furs for more supplies. Mr. Hale also had the distinction of being the first postmaster in Wells County. Receipts for the first three months' operation were twenty-five cents.

Draining the township presented an unusual obstacle. Some rainfall goes directly into the Wabash River, but a greater portion drains into Eight-Mile Creek, flowing northward, and a smaller portion drains into the St. Mary's River on the east.

Ernest Longenberger

Harry Frauhiger (son)

William Frauhiger
(Philip's brother)

Albert Frauhiger
(Philip's son)

August Schlickman

Lewis Yake

Forrest Mankey

Noah Frauhiger
(Philip's son)

Philip Frauhiger

Bertha Frauhiger
(Philip's wife)

Nettie Mankey
(Philip's daughter)

Emma Schlic
(Philip's daug

Fanna Frauhiger
(Philip's daughter)

Della Yake
(Philip's daughter)

Esta Frauhiger
(Noah's wife)

Friends and neighbors often helped out with barn raisings. The Philip Fraughiger barn pictured here was built mainly by relatives and is still standing on the Adams/Wells County line one-half mile south of U.S. 224.

Over the years, Lancaster Township has developed into a prosperous farming community. The portion of the township which borders Bluffton offers comfortable up-scale housing with many new homes as well as the Parlor City Country Club and the Hickory Hills Golf Course. Christian Care Retirement Community offers individual condominiums, apartments, assisted living, and full time nursing care. Meadowville Health and Rehabilitation Center provides assisted living and rehabilitation therapy.

ACRES ON THE WABASH

Located on State Road 116 four miles north of Bluffton and immediately north of Murray, is an area of the Wabash Nature Preserve that was a gift of Catharine and Roland Maxwell in 1973. It is noted for its wildflowers, which are particularly beautiful in spring. This nature preserve has two wildflowers found at none of the other ACRES nature preserves: Wild Hyaciniths (*Camassia scilloides*) and Shooting Stars (*Dodecatheon meadia*). Trails circle the preserve, following near the Wabash River. A gift from the Wells County Foundation funded the development of parking facilities to permit school children from all three Wells County School Districts to visit the area for botanical research.

SCHOOLS IN LANCASTER TOWNSHIP

The first school in the township, which was also one of the first in the county, was taught by A. B. Waugh in a cabin constructed of round logs with greased paper used for windows. The township was among the first in the county to take advantage of an 1816 Indiana law which made possible a free public school system.

Three trustees were elected and eleven schoolhouses were built beginning in 1847. School districts were laid out beginning in the north-east corner of the township with No. 1 known as the Daily School, No. 2 as the Eagleville School, No. 3 as the Donaldson School, No. 4 in the southwestern part of the township, No. 5 as the Center School, No. 6 as the Bender School, No. 7 as the Wasson School, No. 8 as the Toll Gate School, No. 9 as the Lamb School, No. 10 as the Little School, and No. 11 as the Craigville School. In 1856 it was decided that No. 4 was too small and a new district was made for the Murray School. The last district was in the northeast part of the township and was known as the Swamp or Littlevine School.

In 1853 a tax levy in the amount of fifty cents on each $100 valuation was established to build the above schoolhouses. The average bid for each schoolhouse was $352, a pittance when compared to today's multi-million dollar school buildings. These wooden buildings were later replaced with brick structures.

The one-room schools were heated with either a pot-bellied stove or box stove, usually located in the center of the room with the stovepipe suspended with wire as it curved to the nearest wall and ceiling. Wood was the only fuel used. Students sitting farthest away from the stove were permitted to stand around the stove to warm themselves on very cold days. Coats were hung in the vestibule and shelves held lunch pails and water buckets. Both were often frozen on winter days.

All students drank from the same water bucket using either a long handled dipper or tin cups. Parents, realizing the unsanitary conditions of the schools,

The Craigville School class third and fourth grades during the 1927–1928 school year. This school was built in 1895.

A street scene in Craigville around 1900.

required their children to wear asafetida bags to ward off the germs. Rail fences along the way to school made good storage places for the asafeteda bags during the day with the bags being picked up to wear home in the evening. One lady described their odor as being enough to raise your hat when the bags were warmed with body heat.

An academy started by the Rev. Wilson M. Donaldson in Murray in 1852 had as its students George E. Gardiner, Sam Ogden, Henry McLellan, R. F. Gavin, Mary Cotton, A. H. Metts, and others. Joseph Sterling from Pennsylvania was the principal. The academy continued until the time of the Civil War when it suspended operations. The building later was used as a barn on the McCleery farm. The Murrary school was erected in 1899 when Nelson Stafford was trustee. The Craigville school was built in 1895 with Andrew Reed as trustee. Lancaster Central High School, built in 1922, not only stands today but is still used as an elementary school in the Northern Wells School District system. At one time the township was serviced by two steam railroads and one interurban line, the sum of which aided the rapid development of the area.

CORYVILLE/CURRYVILLE

Just a mile east of Craigville was found the village of Curryville, which was also called Coryville. It was platted on the Philip Drum farm by John Philip Drum and Peter Cory. The first church erected in the village was the United Brethren Church, built in 1877.

In 1880, when the Cloverleaf Railroad was constructed, J. P. Drum deeded a right-of-way through his farm, reserving the right to erect an elevator and warehouse later, and a switch was established. This was later torn out and then rebuilt around 1910 for the Erie Stone Company. Later it was once more torn out but was reestablished to allow the farmers to ship grain as well as for the convenience of the St. Louis Sugar Company, which was shipping sugar beets from the locale. Amos Gerber recalled when Curryville housed many Mexican immigrants who came to work on sugar beet farms and in the sugar factory in Adams County. By 1896, the Drum Brothers sawmill was sold to Baron and Warn because of a shortage of timber. In 1907, the Burke elevator was moved across the county line into Adams County. Today Curryville is only a memory, and the Cloverleaf Railroad has long since ceased operation.

CRAIGVILLE

Craigville traces its origin back to April 21, 1879, at the time of the completion of the Cloverleaf Railroad. It was laid out on land belonging to Peter Hetrick and William Hartman. Its name was derived from that of William Craig, a former clerk of the court of Wells County and at that time receiver for the railroad.

The post office was established on April 29, 1879, with John Crist as postmaster. George W. Drum was named postmaster May 15, 1879. Craigville is one of the few small towns in Wells County to still have a post office.

One of two banks to survive the depression in Wells County had its origins in Craigville. Gideon Gerber, father of Amos Gerber, was a farmer and first manager of the elevator in Craigville. He got the community together and sold stock to form the Farmer's State Bank of Craigville. No one was permitted to own more than ten shares when the bank was formed. When the depression occurred, they found it necessary to move the bank to Bluffton in 1933 to survive, and it was rechartered as the Farmers and Merchants Bank. It is still in existence, but has been bought out by Norwest and, more recently, by Wells Fargo.

Amos Gerber recalled the community as it was in the 1920s. Then there was the elevator, a blacksmith shop owned by Aaron Minger, a cheese factory, a stockyard, an auto repair garage, a tile factory at the east end of town, a shoe and harness repair shop, a stepladder factory, and a doctor's office. The restaurant, operated by Frank Diehl, and barber shop, with Harvey Ginther as barber, were housed in the same building. William Diehl had a combined meat market and grocery store in Craigville in his building which had formerly housed the A. L. Brentlinger restaurant. Joel Kaehr had the grocery on the east side of the street, which was also the location of the brick bank building. In the early 1900s, a price

The Craigville depot of the Nickel Plate Railroad about 1920. The Cloverleaf Railroad operated this line originally.

This building housed Frank Deihl's lunch room on the left and Harvy Ginther's barber shop on the right. Harvey Ginther is standing on the left with his daughter Ester Ginther Pease and Glennis Bernes Gerber, who was employed in the lunch room, on the right.

The before and after. Frank Deihl's building as it stands today.

war was waged between the restaurants competing for business. Other businesses were operated by Adam Ritchey, Arthur Brentinger, and Ben John.

Ed and Elmer Moser had the first garage in town. The Mosers developed and built a machine that could mount heavy tractor tires on large tractor wheels. The Craigville garage continues today mainly as an appliance store owned by Daniel Hunt, who is trying to preserve the town's heritage by collecting relics of the town's history. He is also the owner of the Gerber Bank Block building on the south side of the main street across from the garage.

Craigville was the first small town in the county to have street lights. This was due to the efforts of Gideon Gerber, and the willingness of the citizens to pay twenty-five to fifty cents a month for the illumination.

The railroad depot, built when the town was platted in 1879, is now in New Haven, Indiana, as part of the New Haven and Lake Erie narrow-gauge steam railroad.

The four-room school building was built in 1903 and housed grades one through eight plus two years of high school classes. The high school classes were moved to Lancaster High School when it was constructed in 1922.

A survivor, the Craigville Telephone Company, is a family-operated stockholder-owned firm with Howard Reinhard in charge. It has been in business for a century, serving an area overlapping into Adams County and Harrison township in Wells County. Howard Reinhard's father-in-law operated the company before him. This company provided telephone service to some homes even before they had electric service. In addition to Hunt's appliance store mentioned above and the Craigville Telephone Company, existing businesses are the Helena Chemical Company, the diesel repair shop, and the Meyer Building Corporation.

EAGLEVILLE

Eagleville, a mile north of Murray, was laid out by William J. Kirkpatrick, on November 18, 1854. At one time the town had a notions store, a grocery, and a sawmill. It failed to develop into a thriving community as it was located neither on a rail line nor on a major road.

FOX

Little is known of the village of Fox except that the post office was established on February 23, 1859, with William H. H. Reigel as postmaster. It was discontinued on April 1, 1879, and then reestablished briefly on March 10, 1880, with Christopher Hege as postmaster. It was finally discontinued in November 1880.

MURRAY

The town of Murray was laid out and platted October 17, 1839, by Jesse Gerhard. It was enlarged with W. H. Deam's addition July 2, 1853, and Matthew's addition, April 16, 1855. The first commercial enterprise was a store operated by Bowen Hale. His business consisted mainly of trading trinkets, food, and clothing for pelts, which were sent by wagon to Cincinnati or Dayton, Ohio; more commodities were then returned for continued trading. Mr. Hale was also the first postmaster in Wells County, his place of business serving as the first post office. Receipts for the first three months operation of the post office were reported to be twenty-five cents, which is less than the price of one stamp today.

Murray was a strong contender for being selected as the county seat of Wells County. The first settler in the county, Dr. Knox, made his home near Murray, as did many of the other early residents of the county. On the other hand, John Studabaker, Robert Bennett, and Daniel Miller, who owned property along the Wabash River where Bluffton is now located, were determined that the county seat should be there. Studabaker and Bennett even added $270 to their offer of land upon which to lay out the town.

The commissioners appointed to select the county seat were Zachariah Smith of Adams County, Christopher Hanna of Jay County, Champion Helvey of Huntington County, John Rogers of Allen County, and William Kizer of Randolph County. When the commissioners met on the first Monday in March 1848, Zachariah Smith was absent, and the vote for the county seat was tied, two to two. Miller rode off, braving ten inches of snow and following the Wabash River through the dense forest to return with Mr. Smith just in time for the final vote the next morning. As expected, Zachariah Smith cast his vote for Bluffton.

One of the early stores in Craigville, the Abbott and Reed General Store about 1900.

The Ed Kolter and Sam Gerber grocery store on West Market Street directly behind the present day Hunt Appliance Store.

John Gotterly's huckster wagon delivered goods to the fortunate rural homes.

This was to have a decisive effect on the future of Murray.

The town is situated on the north bank of the Wabash River, and was at one time a bustling village. Commercial interests were represented by Lewis F. Shreve, who ran a dry goods store; Peter Clemence and George C. Webber, who had shoe shops; the Webber and Harnish drug store; and J. N. Fink, who was the blacksmith. J. C. Sutton was the local physician. Stafford and Eversole's gristmill, the first in Wells County, was first built in 1837 by Jesse Gerhard. It had two runs of burrs and was powered by water. It continued in operation until August 16, 1907. George Ditzler and Peter Clemence opened the sawmill, which was later operated by L. I. Staver using a twenty-horsepower engine. Murray lagged behind when Bluffton was chosen as county seat. Development was also impeded early on by the lack of railroad facilities.

The Bluffton *Banner*, July 7, 1876, describes the Union Pole raising at Murray. The county's earliest pioneer, Henry Miller, originated and successfully executed the idea of the Union Pole—a pole that would be the emblem of neither political party, but which the citizens of the vicinity could join in raising as a symbol of the love all felt for their county and the position the century 1776-1876 had given the United States among the nations of the earth. A large group of people were on hand on the evening of July 3, 1876, to take part. Music was furnished by the Murray Cornet Band and Plessinger's Martial Band. As the pole reached a vertical position, Capt. E. B. McDowell's artillery company shattered a nearby window glass and "awoke the echoes" with a volley of fire.

One of the most popular picnic grounds was located near Murray on the banks of the Wabash River. It was known as "Boiling Springs," and was the site of many church gatherings, family picnics, and other parties. It is not known if there were actually hot springs in the area, or if the name simply came from the boiling action of the river was it flowed over a rocky bed.

Just one-half mile from the home of the first while settlers, the Reverend Samuel Minnich founded the Murray Christian Church. It was organized with forty charter members in a schoolhouse near the village of Lancaster, as Murray was first known. Charter members were the Gallivans, Millers, Lees, Platters, Nashes, Markleys, and Harveys. Mrs. Elizabeth Harvey, the first white child born in the county, was a deaconess of this church for many years. The Reverend Jennie Jones, the first woman pastor in the county, served this church twice. The Presbyterian Church was dedicated in 1865 by Elder Peter Winchermer.

Pete Wasson's Craigville Grocery and post office circa 1930–1940.

PIGEON ROOST

The northeastern area of the township, which was extremely swampy and marshy, was once inhibited by millions of pigeons. It was said that the pigeons were so numerous they often hid the sun when flying in huge flocks. Men and boys killed the pigeons and carried them away by the wagon-load for the purpose of rendering the fat from them. Obviously, this wholesale destruction soon resulted in the pigeons becoming extinct.

PUGNEY

All that remains of the village of Pugney today is the church, Lancaster Chapel. The Pugney church was one of three churches that were part of a Methodist circuit consisting of Pugney, Tocsin, and Craigville.

VILLA NORTH

Villa North, just as its name indicates, was the village just north of Bluffton, the Wabash River providing a natural boundary. It was first platted as a residential suburb along the west side of the Fort Wayne Road. The Lent A. Williamson house was the first constructed in the addition (1891). Bluffton annexed Villa North in 1965, and the area became a National Register Historic District in 1985.

—B. Elliott

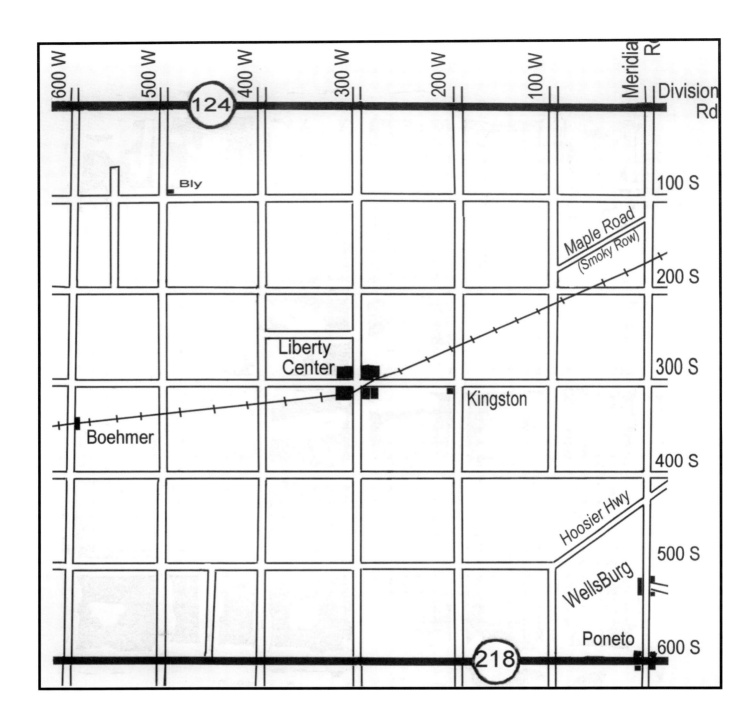

LIBERTY TOWNSHIP

8

When the early pioneers entered Liberty Township they found, as elsewhere in the county, a dense growth of deciduous trees consisting of several varieties of oak, birch, elm, maple, hickory, and walnut. Deer, wildcats, wolves, and small animals were also in abundance. The most plentiful and valuable fruit was the wild blackberry, used for eating and medicinal purposes. Traveling was mainly by horseback and on foot, as there were no wagon trails or roads.

The first settlers in Liberty Township were James Jackson and Henry Mossburg, who arrived in the winter of 1836-1837. They came from Delaware County, where Mr. Mossburg was a minister. It is believed that he was a chaplain in the War of 1812, and his poor health was a result of that service. He died November 2, 1838, and was the first person to be buried in the township. The first white child, born in the township on February 23, 1843, was Sarah First, the daughter of Jacob and his wife.

Others coming in the next few years were G. H. and Johnson King, Davis Chapman, Stuart Bolton, Benjamin Mendenhall, John McFarren, David Goings, George Sparts, George P. Mann, James Merriman, John Hupp, John Muncie, and Jacob and David First. Nine voters were present when the township was organized at the home of Johnson King in April 1842. Because the records were lost, a full list of officers is unknown, but the first trustees were James M. Merriman, John Hoff, and David Goings. Other officers included George P. Mann, clerk; John Hupp, treasurer; James Jackson, supervisor; J. Johnson, justice of the peace; and James Merriman, constable. As soon as the election was settled, the men spent the day log rolling for Mr. King, so as not to waste a day's work.

Originally a part of Rockcreek Township, Liberty Township was the eighth township to be organized in Wells County. Rock Creek drains the six-mile by six-mile township. The first road through the township was surveyed with a pocket compass in 1839 and ran from Bluffton to Jackson Township. Later a road was constructed running directly north and south, bisecting the township at Liberty Center.

BLY

Bly was founded in 1889 and was named after the newspaper reporter, Nellie Bly, who was famous as the first woman to travel around the world. It was eight miles west of Bluffton on the Smoky Row Pike. The latter was so named from the row of cabins lining it, which produced a smoky haze from wood fires. The post office was established in 1890 with Drummond S. Terrell as postmaster and was discontinued in 1902. In October 1908, the entire town was sold to John S. Stroud and Frank C. Dalyrmple and reverted to farm fields.

BOEHMER

Boehmer just grew up on the Huntington—Wells County line and was nameless at first. Since a railroad station was to be located there, it was necessary for the settlement to have a name. It was named after Joseph Boehmer, a bank cashier, who, with Dr. Core Evans, incorporated the Delphos, Bluffton, and

Boehmer, located on the Huntington-Wells County line and on the Delphos, Bluffton, and Frankfort narrow gauge railroad, was a thriving village around 1900.

Frankfort Railroad of Indiana on October 17, 1877. The $30,000 invested by the Wells County Commissioners was nearly enough to build the track of this narrow gauge railroad from Bluffton to Warren. On the day of its completion, the total rolling stock, consisting of an engine, a coach, a boxcar, and six flat-cars, made up the excursion train. Boehmer was surveyed by Jacob Zent on October 8, 1879, but it was not recorded until November 1, 1880.

The plat showed four lots on the north side of the rail-road and ten on the south side. Front Street was the Huntington-Wells County line and parallel to Front Street was Back Street. The first store building was located north of the tracks on the west side of Front Street. It served as a grocery, a dry goods emporium, and the train depot. The first opera-tor of the store was John Neff, a one-armed man who, despite his handicap, also operated a large warehouse. Jim Jones, who ran the saw mill, loaded bridge rafters of oak from a switch south of the tracks and west of Front Street. John Statler operated the blacksmith shop which was in the Wells County part of the village. Early residents were Amos Carroll, whose home was the last to be moved from Boehmer; Ed Gilbert; John Weldon; a Jackson family; William Clannen; Charly and Alice Mossburg; Jimmy Irvin; and Dave Eubanks. At its zenith, the popula-tion of Boehmer was fifty persons.

The Boehmer Methodist Protestant Class was organized by the Rev. E. Robertson on March 29, 1886. Interest was so strong in building a church that $700 was solicited in one day's time. Timber was donated and sawed by Jim Jones in his mill. The church was built by Ves Eiler, with Martin Huggman assisting in finishing the interior and building and dressing the pews. The building was com-pleted in 1888 at a cost of $1800.

In 1886 the railroad, now called the Cloverleaf, changed the road to a stan-dard gauge. The Marion, Bluffton, and Eastern Interurban ran one-half mile north of Boehmer. As railroad business diminished, the automobile took people away from the village, and as was the case with many other Wells County ham-lets, it died peacefully. All that remains today is the church and parsonage.

KINGSTON

Kingston was laid out by the father of Gabriel H. King in 1850 and was in rivalry with Wellsburg. Since it was not located on the railroad, it had little chance for survival and no record of it exists today. It was not even honored with a post office, as most villages were in the 1800s.

LIBERTY CENTER

Liberty Center derives its name from being near the center of Liberty Township. It was platted by John W. Rinear and John Ernst on November 12,

1878, the same year that the Toledo, St. Louis, and Kansas City railroad was built through the area. There were three stores, two sawmills built by Charles Cole and Jacob Jones, blacksmith and wagon shops, a tile factory operated by Adams and Plank, a physician, and a post office. In 1882, G. H. King and Sons erected at flour mill which produced forty-nine barrels per day and was later succeeded by a Garrett and Funk establishment. A tile mill owned by S. J. and J. U. Jackson at one time made up to 15,000 rods of tile per year, quite a capacity for the 1880s. Stores included general stores, (one operated by Johnson and Morgan and one by C. F. Markley); dry goods and groceries (one operated by Miller and Stall and one by Henry King); the Garret and Funk drug store; the Benjamin Foreman shoe store; William Smith's shoe shop; and two broom factories (one operated by Haumesser and Funk and the other by Ramsey and Stall). H. J. Johnson was the barber and Mrs. Marie Turpin ran the Heckman House, built by H. H. Heckman in 1880. Dr. F. W. Garrett served as the town's physician from 1889 until his death in 1923. If your horse needed shoeing, one of the four black-smiths could help you out. They were Mr. Laudermilk, Al Johnson, Isaac Ruth, and Jacob Jones.

The Liberty Center Telephone Company was organized in 1904, providing telephone service throughout the township and into other unserved areas. It was owned by local stockholders, and although it suffered during the Depression, the Liberty Center exchange is still in existence under different management. The Farmers' Grain Company was organized in 1913 and elevator service continued until the demise of rail service. Likewise, the Brady Brothers Stockyard was a bustling business which was later bought out and closed. At one time, the Liberty Center State Bank was a thriving enterprise, as were most small town banks. And, as with most small-town banks, it folded during the Depression. The building was later used for a hatchery.

Main Street (300 West) looking south in Liberty Center in 1910. The Toldeo, St. Louis, and Kansas City Railroad depot is to the left.

Liberty Center School 1911

Liberty Center High School was the source of much controversy when constructed in 1902–1903. This view was taken in 1911.

John Rinear is known by long-time residents as the father of Liberty Center. He moved with his father from Cleveland, then to Huntington County, and finally to Liberty Township where they cleared 120 acres of farmland. At the age of eighteen he enlisted in the 47th Indiana Infantry to fight in the Civil War. He was wounded in the right arm and sent home. On April 2, 1863, he was married to Sarah C. First. Initially they lived on a farm owned by Dr. Melshimer, but later bought forty acres, part of which comprised a portion of Liberty Center. Sarah, who was the first white child in Liberty Township, was the mother of the first white child in Liberty Center, Hannah S. Rinear, who married John B. Funk. John Rinear held every township office except that of assessor. He later was elected to the Indiana State Senate and the Wells County Council, and served as a trustee of the Soldiers' Home at Lafayette.

Liberty Center's first school was made of logs and was replaced later by a frame building. In 1878 a brick building was constructed which consisted of two stories, one room on each floor, at a total cost of $2,700. W. A. Luce, with the assistance of two others, conducted this school during the summer months with an attendance of about thirty pupils. This was replaced by a four-room building in 1896. In 1902 the high school was organized, with the first graduate being Minnie Bundy, an Indian girl. The construction of the high school was the source of much controversy as to the proper site and size. There was much opposition to the addition of an auditorium, but it proved later to be the center of social activities of the community and even served as a study hall. In 1930, Liberty Center

Lake Erie and Western Railroad Depot built in the 1870s in Poneto. Bicycling to the station and then taking the train north or south was a popular means of travel. Just how did they keep those long skirts from tangling in the bicycle chain?

Market Street looking north in Poneto. The Farmers State Bank, which was in business from 1912 until it failed during the depression of 1931, is to the right and John Hardwege's meat market is on the left.

had both grade and high schools while the Bly school and Poneto school were both grade schools. Liberty Township schools were consolidated into the Southern Wells School District in 1962.

Sixteen charter members gathered under an elm tree in June 1856 to form the Liberty Center Baptist Church. Charter members were the Johnsons, Parkers, Rinears, Spakes, Merrimans, Mounseys, Irvins, and Jacob First. A brick church, constructed in 1883, was destroyed by a storm in 1896 and replaced by the present building.

Both Liberty Methodist and Boehmer Methodist had their beginnings in the Salamonie circuit. The Rev. J. C. Macklind organized both churches in 1887. In 1876 John Mounsey asked George Hubbard, who lived northwest of Warren, to hold services in south Liberty Township. Although the congregation was formed in 1877, it was housed in the Mounsey schoolhouse until 1886 when a church was built on the northwest corner of Section 32. Pastor Macklind and some members went to the woods, cut the timber, and completed the church on February 17, 1888, at the cost of $1,000. The 35x50 foot frame building was heated by two wood stoves. Some of the original timbers are still in the old mill building formerly owned by the Farmers' Grain Company, which used the original church when a new cement block structure was built in 1907.

At one time a busy center of commerce and social life, today Liberty Center is a sleepy crossroads with a fire station, a small convenience store and a couple of gas pumps, and two very active churches. Social activities center around these churches and the Southern Wells school activities.

PONETO

Poneto could rightfully have been placed in this account with either Harrison or Liberty Township, since it straddles both townships. It has been placed with Liberty, as its early ties appeared to be more closely related to Liberty Center and

125

Ben and Ellen Holsinger in front of the Poneto Lumber Company in the 1930s. The lumber yard was located strategically near the railroad.

W. B. Jones and Son blacksmith is seen on the left of this view of Poneto. Passengers are boarding the interurban to travel either north to Bluffton or south to Hartford City or Muncie.

Liberty Township than to Harrison, and geographically more of its area lies in Liberty than Harrison Township.

Poneto was platted as Worthington on September 4, 1871, by Simeon Tappy. It became a station on the L. E. and W. (Lake Erie and Western) railroad. Today it is a crossing for the busy Norfolk and Western Railroad. Poneto was in competition with Wellsburg, which was just north of Poneto and also on the Liberty/Harrison Township line, for the privilege of being the railway stop. First named Worthington, after the superintendent of the railroad, its name was later changed to Poneto in 1880 when it was learned that another town with the name Worthington already existed.

One source related that Poneto was the name of an Indian camp west of the town and referred to the eating of corn pone. Another source states that three persons each selected a syllable and then put the three together to obtain a name which was not claimed by any other town in the whole world.

In its early days Poneto was a village with a post office, two stores, a blacksmith, a wagon shop, two sawmills, a tile factory, and two physicians. The post office was first established as Worthington Crossing on October 19, 1870, with William Singer as postmaster. When the town was platted in 1871, the only building was Mr. Tappy's residence and a sawmill owned by Dr. C. T. Melsheimer. A large brick business block was originally built by John Hardwidge in 1881 and later enlarged. The S. M. King saw, planing, and corn-feed mills were built in 1881. Charles McAdams opened his grocery in January of 1907. In 1908 the Burgess brothers bought the local furniture store and Simon Foreman purchased the general store. Mr. Kimmell opened a new restaurant in 1910. Frank Fryer's drug store was destroyed by fire in 1909, with an estimated loss of more than $4,000. Local citizens were pleased when Henry Gaught bought the

mitten factory from George Slinger and E. H. Collins and increased wages. The oil boom in the area, which began in the early 1890s, also resulted in a new Snyder Hotel opening in 1909. Like many other small towns located near or in the oil and gas field, Poneto was a lively place around the turn of the century and was the location of many saloons. New sidewalks were even installed in 1905.

Important to the early history of Poneto was the Bank of Poneto, organized by Abner Chalfant, the grandson of Chads Chalfant, who had brought his family to the southwest quarter of Section 25 in 1837. The family, including Chads's son Reason, accumulated a considerable fortune, making it possible to underwrite the bank formation. The Farmers State Bank was founded in March 1912, with J. W. Cook as president and W. A. Popejoy as vice president. Both banks were victims of the Depression years.

One of the big attractions of Poneto was the race track. The track was on the farm of Dr. Hezakiah Doster, just south of one of his fish ponds. His son-in-law, Dr. Francis Buckner, was one of the most avid horseman involved with the track. Others included Tom Thea, Cyrus Stine, and a Mr. McCarvey. The track served as training quarters for a number of horses. About the same time, the Poneto Street Fair was an exciting event drawing large crowds to the small town.

The Poneto School was originally split into separate winter and spring sessions. These were combined finally to form one seven-month term. Around the turn of the century, it was common for students to attend high school in Bluffton, living with relatives, friends, or boarding out. They spent their vacations and weekends at home, if travel was possible. Poneto was not without culture, however. The Literary and Debating Society had a hard time of it, and according to the Bluffton *Banner*, went "dunk" in 1896. The Red Men's Lodge was active in Poneto, and moved their "Wigwam" from the Hardwedge Building to the William Allyn Building. Frank Hardwedge owned the "opera hall." The Odd Fellows Lodge was organized June 30, 1899. Around 1920 it was reported that the Odd Fellows numbered more than 100 members. The auxiliary of the I. O. O. F., the Order of the Rebakahs, was also organized at Poneo and active in the community.

Today Poneto is still on a busy rail line and, as a result, is the site of a large agricultural operation owned by the Anderson Company. Not even a service station is operated there today, but there is a car repair service on the site of a defunct station. The town still maintains a fire house and an operating post office serving the rural area of southern Wells County. The Poneto Methodist church is still active in the area. Depending upon the township in which they live, students attend either the Bluffton-Harrison or Southern Wells school system.

The Poneto Hardware served as the post office from 1914 to 1920.

WELLSBURG

Wellsburg is also a forgotten town of the past. One source says it was located two miles north of Poneto. According to legend, it derived its name from the fact that it was laid out by a relative of William Wells, for whom the county was named. Amos Davis served as the first postmaster when the post office was established in 1870. The post office, however, was discontinued in 1873.

—*B. Elliott*

The Cook and Green garage in 1911. Note the gas pump and the air pump in the background and the single advertisement "car." There was ample space for repair considering the number of autos in service at that time.

The Bank of Poneto, organized by Abner Chalfant, was a financial mainstay in the area from 1912 to 1923.

Elda Burnau and Harold Hott in front of their place of employment, the Smith Garage.

UBLIC SCHOOL — PONETO, IND.

The Poneto Public school was constructed in 1911 and served the community for many years. Later children attended either Liberty Center, Bluffton, Petroleum, or Jackson high schools depending on where they lived. Today they attend either Bluffton-Harrison or Southern Wells schools.

The Methodist Church is still an active component of the Poneto community today.

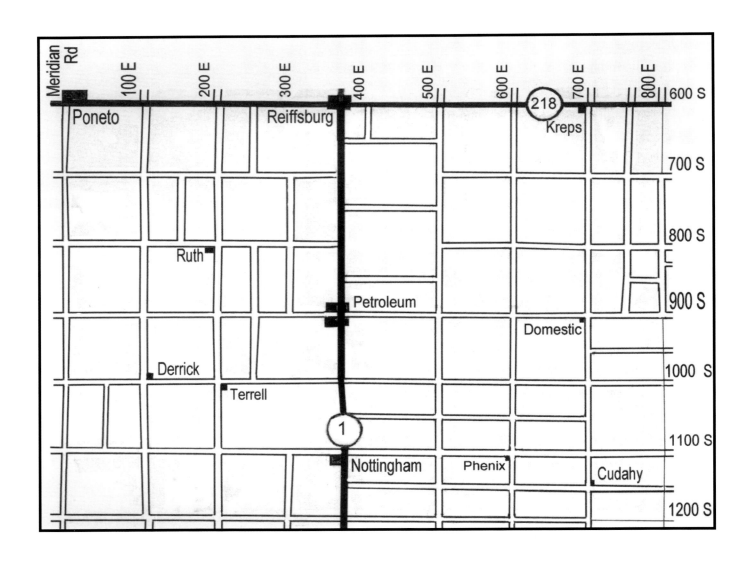

NOTTINGHAM TOWNSHIP

9

Nottingham Township is said to have derived its name from Nottingham, England. The township was set aside from Harrison Township by the Board of Commissioners on January 4, 1841, being the fifth of Wells County's nine townships. With its dense forestation and distance from water transportation, the land wasn't settled as early as other parts of the county.

The first election in the township was held on the first Monday in April of that year, in the Hite cabin in section 14. Fifteen votes were cast, resulting in the election of the following officers: Jacob Warner, Gabriel Burgess, and George Sowers, trustees; Abraham Stahl, clerk and treasurer; and Jacob Warner, supervisor. Prior to this time, Jacob Warner had been supervisor of an eight-mile-square district in the original Harrison Township.

FIRST SETTLERS

Joseph Blackledge from Baltimore, Maryland, built the first log cabin, establishing his home in 1837. As it was typical in other areas of the county at that time, his home was surrounded by forest, far from civilization, and distant from the nearest neighbor. In 1838, other families arrived—John Dawson, Lyman Bass, Hezekiah Grimes, Peter Garner, Abram Stahl, John and William Nutter, Isaac and Edward Haynes, and Robert Smith.

Jacob Warner with his wife and a child arrived the same year from Pickaway County, Ohio. Their trip took seven days. He had purchased 160 acres from the government before moving. After his arrival, he bought another eighty acres for two young men who assisted him in clearing his farm. The first year they were able to clear a fifteen-acre field, which was planted with two bushels of seed corn and a bushel of seed potatoes brought from Ohio.

Going to the mill at Winchester, Indiana, to have the corn ground into meal was a laborious trip. Neighbors joined together for the trip, which required clearing a trail through the forest. The only meat was deer and only if game was killed with a rifle.

John K. Reiff was born in Berks County, Pennsylvania, in 1799 and came to Nottingham Township with his wife Susanna and eleven children in 1840. Their nearest neighbor was two miles distant. Deer and turkeys were plentiful for food and, with corn bread, this sustained his family.

These first settlers witnessed the growth of the township from the time it was a wilderness, dotted with Indian wigwams, to the days when it became a prosperous agricultural community. When Nottingham Township was settled, the Indians were at peace with the whites. With little trouble from the Indians, the opening up and settlement of the township went unmolested.

The first work for the pioneer's family was to build a cabin. Trees of uniform size were felled and cut into the desired length, usually twelve to fifteen feet, and hauled to the selected home site. Neighbors would assemble on an appointed day for a "cabin raising." By nightfall, the little cabin would be up and ready for a "house warming," when music, dancing, and other festivities would be enjoyed. Light was provided by burning hickory bark or lard placed in a tea cup with a wick made of cloth.

Among the early settlers was the Philip Alberson family, pictured here in front of their cabin.

The spinning wheel was a necessity in nearly every home and at least one loom would be found in the neighborhood serving the needs of several families. Flax was spun into thread, then woven on the loom into a long-wearing jeans material. Sheep were raised for their wool, which was sheared and colored in an iron kettle filled with water and walnut bark, a process that would take several weeks. After the wool had dried, burrs and dirt were picked out. The wool was then carded, either by hand, or if available, with a carding machine. Later the women in the home would spin it into threads on the "big wheel."

Food was limited to cornbread, hominy or "samp" (a boiled cereal made from hominy), beans, pumpkin, venison, pork, turkey, prairie chicken, squirrel, and other game, with a few vegetables raised during the summer months. Wild blackberries were a staple food of the time, with large patches located in Nottingham. One patch was calculated to contain 320 acres. Wild plums and wild cherries were also plentiful.

Wild hogs were numerous. These were hogs that had strayed or been left behind by discouraged settlers. The "poll wood" was a great haunt for these wild hogs and other game. It was a strip of trees and vines, commencing south of Poneto and extending along the north side of the township, running across Adams County to the Ohio state line. Deer were killed here in great numbers, and in the fall, when the wild hogs had fattened on acorns and other nuts, people would come with horse-drawn sleds and butchering kettles to kill their winter meat supply.

BEGINNING ENTERPRISE

The people's needs were much the same. All were working to establish schools, churches, drainage ditches, roads, post offices, mills, and trading posts.

An iron kettle over an open fire had many uses through the year. George L. Warner relaxes as he stirs the apple butter made by his wife Suzanna.

The rapid immigration of pioneer families brought enterprising men forward to establish trading posts and build saw mills as well as mills for grinding corn into meal and wheat into flour. A local mill saved days and even weeks of difficult travel to Winchester, Richmond, or Fort Wayne, for there were no roads or even trails to those places. Often there were swollen streams to cross as well. One of the first mills in the area was built on the Salamonie River, near Montpelier. In 1843–44, Joshua Bond built a grain mill in Penn Township, Jay County. Horsepower was used to power this mill. The farmers would take one or two sacks of grain on horseback, with a second horse in harness to help power the mill.

SCHOOLS ORGANIZED

The first school was held in a rude log cabin located in section 11. Taught by Mrs. Mary King, the school was private, paid for by subscription. Nottingham was the first township in the county to establish its school districts. The first public school was opened here in 1850. An election was held for school purposes in 1849 when Stanton Scott, instrumental in encouraging education, became trustee-treasurer and Jason B. Blackledge was named trustee-clerk. If a district had a sufficient number of scholars, a district trustee (later a district school director) was appointed. Other men active in school affairs in that period were Gabriel Burgess, E. Harlin Phillips, Samuel Watts, Samuel Hurst, James S. Williams, John Dawson, Henry King, John K. Reiff, Alonzo Lockwood, Abram Stahl, Stephen Prouty, and James Green. A school enumeration, taken in 1849, the first school year, listed 149 pupils in the township's nine school districts. Three years later, the count was 168. A teacher's pay in that period was typically $20 per year plus room and board.

Petroleum High School was built in 1899, with Samuel Gehrett as trustee. With later additions, the building became the consolidated school for all grades, replacing the twelve district school buildings.

ROADS

The first travel routes were the old Indian trails. One running through Nottingham Township extended from Richmond to Winchester and Pennville, then on to Bluffton and Fort Wayne. State Road 1 follows this route today through Wells County.

The first roads were cut through the forest by settlers between homes, with each family clearing their own route. In 1854, roads were being laid out in straight lines, but the first roads between houses were still used to a great extent where rail fences had not been built.

At least three months of the year, and sometimes as much as five months, it was impossible for the farmers to get to town with their wagons. Many times it was necessary to have a yoke of oxen or two horses to pull a wagon through the mud and over corduroy road stretches (split log or plank) when hauling only two

Oil well drilling in 1900 was done at a frantic pace with little concern for neatness. Drillers worked long hours to sink as many wells as possible on their leased land.

The derrick on the Sterling Blocker farm was set for drilling in 1919.

sacks of wheat—a necessary trip to have the wheat ground into flour for the family. During periods of freezing weather and with snow on the ground, a sled could be used to carry the produce to market. Although corduroy roads were an improvement, it was not until gravel roads were built that general economic progress was made.

DITCHES AND DRAINAGE

Farmers realized the need for artificial drainage at the very beginning, because of the extensive wetlands. As early as 1845, public ditches were petitioned for, as provided by state law. The western portion of Nottingham Township is drained by Rock Creek and its contributing ditches while Six Mile Creek drains the eastern portion. The largest tile drains petitioned for in the township are the George B. Schott ditch (two and a half miles long, with cement tile ranging from eight to twenty-four inches in diameter) and the P. B. Alberson ditch (three miles long, with cement tile from eight to twenty-two inches in diameter).

William Kirkwood of Nottingham served as the first drainage commissioner of Wells County under the state statute whereby ditches could be established by petition through the circuit court.

CHURCHES

The first settlers met in their various homes to conduct religious services. Later services were held in the log school houses, the first of which was built in 1849. By 1867 the need for a community house of worship was felt, and the United Brethren Church was built in 1870. This was a frame building, thirty-five by forty-five feet, with a seating capacity of five hundred. Jacob Warner, Amos Garrett, and John Shigley were its first church trustees and the Reverend Samuel Neher was the first pastor. Another United Bretheren Church was built at Phenix in 1875. It had a seating capacity of three hundred. In 1876 the Christian Church with seating of four hundred was built. The Evangelical Association Salem Church, first organized in 1854 with a membership of thirty, met first in the Sauer home and then in the Lindsey schoolhouse. Next they met at the Father Kreps home until 1855, when a small frame building became their new home. A new church building was erected in 1877.

The Methodist Episcopal Church erected a frame building in Reiffsburg, seating 250. The building was dedicated August 8, 1880, during the pastorate of the Reverend H. C. Myers. The Airline Methodist Episcopal Church was established in 1890 in a frame building moved from the edge of Adams County. The Airline trustees at that time were Amos Sawyer, John Henley, and Joseph Risser. During the oil boom days and the founding of Petroleum, the United Bretheren built their church there in 1897.

OIL BOOM DAYS

The discovery of natural gas, just to the east near Findlay, Ohio, in the 1880s, brought prospectors and drillers to southern Wells County. Nearly every ten acres had a well drilled on it. An Indiana Department of Conservation map dated 1962, attested to the fact that this Wells County area contained more oil and gas wells than any other area of the state. By 1904, more than 20,000 bores had been made in a four hundred-square-mile area that included Wells County, and most of them were producers of gas and/or oil. All of this activity took place before the oil discoveries in Texas and Oklahoma.

Initial drilling for gas provided an abundance that was considered at the time to be inexhaustible. Drillers let excess natural gas burn off, and excursion trains brought crowds to see the strange sights of towers of flame. It was estimated that the waste was some one hundred million cubic feet per day. Gas production dropped by the late 1890s. In 1890, a major oil strike was made near Keystone in Chester Township. Thus the oil boom began. Opportunity knocked with the presence of a growing number of oil workers, and John W. Bears opened his general store in 1893. Petroleum came onto the map as the state's newest boomtown.

George Warner, a lifelong resident of Petroleum, born in 1921, was interviewed by the *Indianapolis Star* for an article in their Sunday, July 10, 1994, edition. Referring to the oil wells located around the town, George stated that when he was a boy in the 1920s, "you could hear a 'chug - chug' reverberating across the countryside as the engines pumped oil from the wells." The "chug" came from the "barkers" put on the engines by the oil pumpers so they could tell from a distance their engines were running. A barker was a pipe device mounted on the engine's exhaust pipe. When the exhaust hit the open end of the pipe it made a loud barking sound that could be heard for miles. Each barker had its own distinctive sound. Oil from the wells flowed through pipes stretching across the land; farmers were willing to farm around the obstructions that put money in their pockets for every barrel

Crops were planted around the wells. This was one of several on the Howard Yarger farm, connected by pull rods and powered by one engine.

One of the last general stores in Wells County was operated by Francis and Addie Cochran from 1918 to its closing in 1979. The store was first opened in 1889, and included the Phenix post office.

of oil pumped. He remembered his father's stories about how "shooting a new well had to be one of the more exciting events of the day. When they were going to shoot a well, they'd get a crowd because the oil and gas would come up right through the derrick," he explained. "They'd put nitro down in the bottom of the well and then drop in what they'd call a 'go-devil,' a piece of metal. When it hit that nitroglycerine a thousand feet down, why, it would explode and shatter the rock and let the oil come in more freely."

An immense amount of nitroglycerine was needed for shooting all the wells in the county. Meeting this need was a nitroglycerine plant, a mile east of Bluffton, located a half mile north of State Road 124 on County Road 400 East. From this site, it was hauled by horses and wagon to the drilling sites. The Harrison Township section of this book recalls the story of a disastrous explosion of a horse-drawn wagonload of nitroglycerine.

TOWNS

Nottingham is recognized as the oldest village in the township. Named after the township, it remained a small crossroads village until its demise in the 1940s, when most of the country's small-town general stores, banks, barber shops, and other small businesses lost their customers to the cities' larger markets. Samuel Watts provided postal service from his crossroad home, serving as postmaster as early as 1849. Mail arrived then twice a week from Winchester and Huntington. The oil wells drilled and operated in southern Wells County in the 1890s brought a population growth that led to the platting of town lots in Nottingham on June 10, 1895.

Domestic, first called Ringville, had a post office established in 1884. Although it is listed on some road maps today, the grocery store operated by Emma Blocher for many years no longer exists.

Cudahy, named for the Cudahy Oil Company which drilled many of the oil wells in the area, appeared as a crossroads village in 1896, but was not platted.

Kreps was named for John Kreps, who established a store on his land in 1890. There was once a sawmill located here as well as the Kreps School. Old Salem Church is nearby.

Phenix (a variant spelling of Phoenix) was established in 1889 with a post office. The old store building is still standing, but in poor condition. Francis Cochran and his wife Addy ran this store, purchased from Willy Alberson in 1918. After Francis died in 1954, his wife continued operating the store until it was closed in 1979. A huckster wagon from the store toured the area, bringing groceries and general merchandise to the farm families. Eggs and farm produce were traded for store goods. For many years Francis threw an annual Halloween party that drew people from miles around. Prizes were given for the best costumes. This was great fun for the community and probably reduced the number of destruc-

Huckster wagons from towns throughout Wells County were frequently seen on the roads, the first ones pulled by teams of horses. This 1927 Chevrolet truck from the Phenix store would stop at farm homes, where the farm wife traded eggs, butter, chickens, and garden produce for things not produced on the farm.

The highest point in Petroleum was atop the grain elevator. The elevator had to close with the loss of a railroad connection when the CB&C Railroad failed in 1917. It was moved to Poneto, on the Fort Wayne to Muncie Railroad.

tive acts that sometimes occur at that time of year.

Derrick (1897), Ruth (1889), and Terrell (1890), were other villages in Nottingham Township that came on the scene as a result of the oil boom. These new towns experienced an influx of oil workers who brought a bawdy lifestyle that filled the new stores, saloons, and hotels that sprang up. The towns soon suffered with the end of the oil days, and like other small towns, became victims of better roads and the automobile, which eliminated the need for local stores.

PETROLEUM

The arrival of rail service in 1903 with the Cincinnati, Bluffton, and Chicago Railroad, as well as the oil discoveries, did wonders for Petroleum, which

The Cincinnati, Bluffton, & Chicago railroad suffered financially and had one disaster after another with bridge failures, law suits, and an unattended engine backing off the end of the track in Huntington and into a grocery store, where it fell into the basement. Only the front of the engine and smokestack remained visible. The gas-electric car was an attempt to convert the line to a traction system in 1911.

was platted in 1904. The peak of Petroleum's prosperity found two doctors, five general stores, a hotel and a saloon, and two barbers, along with a newspaper in the little town. Nearly every house in Petroleum had gas lights, gas heating, and gas cooking appliances.

Petroleum was the center of considerable oil excitement beginning in the mid-1890s. A post office was established here on January 22, 1894. The Cudahy oil interests (later sold to the Standard Oil Company) were prominent in the exploring, drilling, and pumping of oil in the area. The boom period developed Petroleum into a bustling town, with its own weekly newspaper, *The Petroleum Journal*, touted as "An Independent Newspaper." Its first issue of four pages was dated May 3, 1906. The annual subscription rate was 50 cents. The publisher and proprietor, Walter E. Grant, promised a "small clean paper with plenty of home and country news." This issue carried advertisements for Byron Witmer's "The Old Reliable" General Store; Petroleum Meat Market; Petroleum Grain and Lumber Company; The Buffington Stock Food Company; Schott & Stahly Hardware; J. W. Bears General Store; C. L. White, General Merchandise; C. D. Risser Livery and Feed Barn; and the professional cards of H. W. Markley, MD; F. M. Dickason, MD; and Dr. G. C. Emick, veterinary surgeon and dentist. The tonsorial offered a "nice smooth Shave or an Up to Date Hair Cut." The Cornet Band was "doing fine and expected to give weekly concerts in the summer."

The first issue of the weekly *Petroleum Journal* appeared in 1906. All of the area news and gossip was reported. With a subscription of 50 cents per year, its cost was less than one cent per issue!

THE PETROLEUM JOURNAL
An Independent Newspaper

VOL. I.   PETROLEUM, INDIANA, THURSDAY, MAY 3, 1906.   No. 1

INDIANA STATE NEWS

Indianapolis, April 27.—The supreme court has taken the life out of the drastic anti-cigarette law enact-

School Enumeration

Trustee N. L. Bloxsom has finished the school enumeration for Nottingham township, and there is a decrease over last year of 17. This year there is a total of 2...

Died Suddenly.

Albert E. Irey, living east of Petroleum, died suddenly of peritonitas. He was at town apparently as well as ever on Saturday, but on Sunday at ten o'clock he

NOT A REVOLUTION

Paris Got Over May Day Without Any Change In the Existing Order of Th...

Main Street, Petroleum, looking east in 1910. The large building on the right, the Fisher Building, was built in 1906. Across the street, the building with the balcony is said to have been a hotel.

"The large building belonging to Charles Fisher is being rapidly pushed to completion. It will contain two business rooms below with a large public hall above and will be a fine addition to the town." This news item in the paper detailed an eagerly awaited entertainment center. The second floor hall contained a stage at one end where traveling troops and entertainers would present shows for the community. It was also used as a basketball court. In the lower east room of the building around 1936, a young man named Welker created the concrete tree with a bear and squirrel on its limbs that has been a landmark for over sixty years at the site of the Airplane service station in Bluffton.

Another news item on page one, "Attempt to Steal a Horse," stated "Monday morning at 1:20 as Nate Neff's son drove into the barn he was startled to hear the tread of horses hoofs and to see the form of a man leading one of Mr. Neff's most valuable horses toward the door. As soon as the thief became aware of the son's presence, he released the horse and fled. For some time there has existed an organized band of horse thieves who are thought to have their headquarters in Adams County near Decatur. This fact seems to cast suspicion that the would-be thief is a member of this gang."

The paper also carried local news from Phenix, Nottingham, Balbec, and Fiat, as well as Petroleum.

The failure in 1917 of the Cincinnati, Bluffton, and Chicago Railroad (CB&C, nicknamed "Corn Beef & Cabbage") caused the closing of the Petroleum Elevator and a creamery. The elevator was moved to Poneto, located on the Lake Erie & Western Railroad (LE&W, also referred to as "Leave Early and Walk"). By 1918, there were five stores, a bank, and a garage remaining. The United Brethren Church and the Odd Fellows Lodge provided the religious and social elements of the town.

Before 1920 oil well production faded, and in 1917 the CB&C Railroad, Petroleum's most important link to the outside world, failed. The dream of a rail line from Cincinnati to Chicago through this area only materialized as a single track line in Indiana from Portland to Bluffton to Huntington. During the last days of World War I in 1918, the CB&C engine was shipped to France but never arrived. The ship it was on was sunk somewhere off the coast of Europe by the German navy.

Petroleum, like many small towns in Wells County, had both horseshoe and croquet courts. These games filled many hours of the days during the Depression. With little or no work to be had, croquet took on a special importance with well-attended tournaments between towns. Fifteen cents to enter a contest was a big deal when a day's wages might be only fifty cents.

In 1927, Calvin Risser employed John Bears to build a filling station on his land at the corner of State Road 3 (now State Road 1) and Market Street. The station, operated by Bill Mason, sold Refiners gasoline, candy, pop, and cigarettes. Few cars came by in those days to interrupt the loafers who dropped in every day to talk and play cards, usually Rook. The station changed to Shell gasoline and went through several owners until George Risser, son of Calvin, bought the station in 1946 and operated it until 1967. Before the advent of television, the station was always a favorite meeting place, attracting large crowds of Petroleum residents and neighboring farmers in the evenings. Late in 1948, several cars returning from the last of the season's Purdue football games and a Trailways busload of passengers became snowbound at Petroleum. Forty people spent the night in Risser's Shell Station, waiting for snow plows to open the highway to Bluffton.

In 1928, the same year State Highway 3 (Indiana State Highway 1 today) was paved between Petroleum and Bluffton, and five years before the Indiana State Police were established (in 1933), the Petroleum Bank was robbed and closed its doors forever. As a child coming home from school that day, George Warner said he could hardly believe the report of the robbery. When he looked in the bank's front door, he saw pennies scattered about the floor. How could anyone rob a bank and leave all of those pennies?

During summer weekends in the late 1930s, free movies for the local residents were projected on the back white-painted wall of the grocery/IOOF lodge building. Families brought their blankets to settle down for a great evening of entertainment as soon as darkness fell. Usually the movies were serials—it was a long wait for the next week's installment.

Beverly Stoner Patrick recalls how she and her sister had a job every evening delivering milk to the customers of her grandmother Lovina Risser. The milk from her jersey cows was kept on the back porch in galvanized containers submerged in cold water for keeping until she filled the quart bottles. She sold cream, skimmed from the top of the milk to the creamery, next door to her farm. The girls could then join their friend playing a popular game of "Slip."

—*P. Bender*

Dick Risser at the Petroleum Livery Stable is holding the horse's halter. Harry Risser is seated in the sleigh on the left, ready to drive.

CHAS FISHER RURAL CARRIER READY TO START
DELIVERING MAIL PETROLEM, IND.

Charles Fisher, R.F.D. (Rural Free Delivery) No. 1, Petroleum, faithfully delivered the mail in all kinds of weather, on his appointed rounds, in his fully enclosed wagon. Even the small openings for driving reins were designed for cold weather.

Cold winter weather forced the "regulars" inside for the warmth of the johnny stove. The 1950s crowd at Risser's included (left to right) Donald Williams, Harry Hiday, Ray Kirkwood, Roy Allen, and Ralph Lockwood, kept away from their chores.

The gasoline filling station, such as Risser's in Petroleum, was a favorite place to pass the time of day. Left to right are Brent Nutter, Bert Davenport, Harold "Dutch" Hiday, and Walt Deren. In the 1940s, motor oil was dispensed from quart glass bottles as seen stored beneath the "liar's bench."

The 1941 prices at Ralph and Bernice Baker's grocery in Petroleum were displayed in the store windows. The low prices matched the low wages of the era.

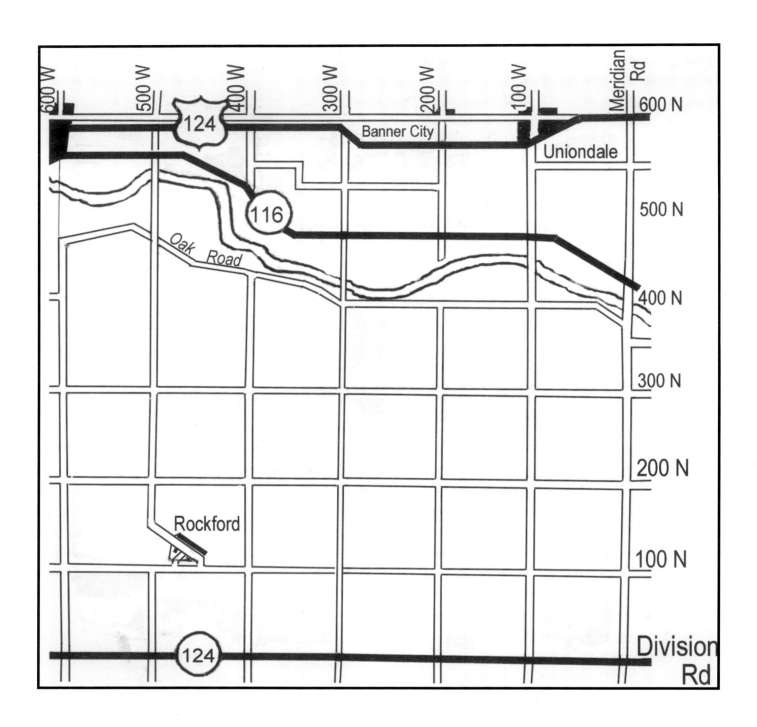

ROCKCREEK TOWNSHIP

10

Rockcreek Township was named after the creek that flows across the township from the south to the northwest and empties into the Wabash River southwest of Markle. Indiana became a state in 1816; twenty-one years later, in July 1837, this township was organized. The name "Rockcreek" originally referred to the entire western half of the county. As the later townships Jackson, Chester, Liberty, and Union were formed out of that land area, Rockcreek retained its name, although it was finally reduced in size. The bed of the creek was solid Niagara limestone, which was useful for building roads and for cementing, as well as providing decorative flagstone. The limestone was also used as fertilizer that was good for reducing the acidity of the soil.

Many ancestors of the present-day residents came from eastern Pennsylvania. Jacob Miller was one of the earliest settlers. In 1835 other settlers were Matt Davis, Solomon Johnson, Benjamin Brown, Soloman Sparks, and Isaac DeWitt. On June 18, 1836, Solomon Johnson was elected county commissioner.

In 1836, William and Allen Redding, Thomas T. Smith, John Zeke, David Snyder, and William Barton arrived. In 1837 Thomas and Samuel Wallace, Mason Powell, and William Ellingham moved to the area. William Redding served this township as trustee and also one year as supervisor.

William Barton was said to have come here from New England in 1836. When he first arrived he took up residence in the hollow of a sycamore tree on the Samuel McAfee farm. According to legend the tree was so large that he could lie down in it, although he was over six feet tall!

Families coming to the township between 1840 and 1870 were the Brickleys, Haiflichs, Newhards, Lipkeys, Leshes, Houtzes, Deckers, Fishbaughs, Lamms, McAfees, Breners, Myers, Crums, Souerwines, and Edrises.

Some of the familiar Scotch and Irish that settled here were the Crosbies, Gordons, Greggs, Grahams, Hoggs, and Storys. They were known as industrious, religious, sociable, and hospitable people who faced the hardships of pioneer life with great determination and resourcefulness.

Close to ninety percent of the people of the township are descendants of German or English ancestors. Their forefathers came here to try to better their living conditions. Many left Germany because of threatening wars, both civil and international, and because of poor economic conditions and the lack of political liberty and religious freedom.

During the summers the chief work was tilling the soil and reaping. During the winters the farmers spent much of their time in the forests clearing more acres for tilling, cutting wood, and splitting logs. A good chopper could split one-hundred rails in a day. The women spent time spinning and weaving. Cornbread, mush and milk, fried mush, and meats like pork, beef, mutton, fish, squirrel, venison, and bear meat were the principal foods. Wheat bread was a luxury for the settlers.

The first election held in the township was on May 8, 1839. At the time, this included what were later Union, Liberty, Chester, Jackson, and Rockcreek townships. Voting took place at the home of Benjamin Brown, the inspector, who was also elected justice of the peace.

Another pair of hands taking the reins was a great help in operating the plow. Here a heavy timber placed on the plow keeps the plowshare in the hard ground.

The first school in the township was Redding School, built in 1838–1839. The first teacher was William Clark. Many log schools were later replaced by painted white frame buildings. Much later, brick schools were built. Jacob Haiflich built the township's first brick school in 1862.

Parents elected the schoolteachers by ballot. Each school had one director who was responsible for keeping up with repairs, selling the wood job to the lowest bidder, and presiding at all school meetings.

Sometimes teachers boarded with different families. Often they didn't receive pay in cash, but in corn, wheat, or chickens. At most, children attended school seven months of the year with many attending for shorter periods. The average class attendance was sixty-five children.

Between 1850 and 1870, teachers who earned one dollar per day were licensed by a school examiner. Beginning in 1852, the township trustee hired and fired teachers, built schoolhouses, bought school supplies, and paid salaries and bills.

Other township schools were Bender School (built in 1878), Miller School, Haiflich School, McAfee or Iron Bridge, Shively, Sugar Grove, Raber, Falk, and Center School. Center School later became Rockcreek Township School in 1922.

Samuel McAfee, a farmer, was named constable of the township in 1848. Later, in 1865, the Rockcreek Township Horse Thief Association was established. Their first leader was Isaac Decker. They met twice a year and were proud of the fact that no member ever had a horse stolen. They disbanded, and within six months three horses had been stolen. Soon they reorganized with Jacob Farling as president, Joseph Lesh as secretary, and W. F. Cotton as treasurer. To belong to the association you had to brand the front hoof of your horse with an R.

The goals of most families in the township were much the same; they worked to establish schools, churches, ditches, roads, post offices, mills, and trading posts. They banded together to meet these and other needs to make the future more promising. Clearing the heavily forested farms and draining their many wetlands were probably the most challenging tasks facing the early settlers.

Most of the pioneer families of this township were large. Diphtheria and scarlet fever frequently turned into epidemics. People died by the score. Very few families escaped these dreaded diseases. Small pox, milk sickness, human cholera, ague, and malaria were other common illnesses.

The first Sunday school was held at the Isaac DeWitt home in 1838. The Reverend Hallet Barber gave the sermon. The Reverend Barber died in 1849 of smallpox. He is buried in Rockford Cemetery.

Although many of the township's residents met together in the 1850s, only a few of the religious groups had organized as churches or had hired preachers to meet with them weekly. Many societies had no church of their own and met in homes or schoolhouses. Slowly, however, they joined a circuit and a church district.

Rockford was also a Quaker settlement. The Quaker meetinghouse organized in 1892, stood adjacent to the Friends Cemetery.

The Rockcreek Methodist Church, was dedicated in 1868. Weekly average attendance was sixty-five members.

The Rockford Reformed Church was three-fourths mile north of town. It had fifty or sixty members, and was dedicated by the Reverend John Naille. The Seventh Day Adventists Church was organized in April 1887. Saint Paul's Church—Reformed and Lutheran was built in 1857. A new church was built in 1880 on land donated by Abram Mast. Sparks Methodist Episcopal Church was in the northern part of the township and had over fifty members. Horeb Lutheran Church, also in the northern part of the township, was built in 1875. Some of its early elders were Joseph Seaman, Randall Schoonover, Jonathan Seaman, and William Scott.

Thomas T. Smith built the first frame house in Rockcreek Township. He died April 4, 1880.

The Rockcreek Township Farmers Mutual Fire Insurance Company was organized in 1875. This was a fund that lent families or businesses money for losses after a fire.

In February 1882, a large bear was killed near the old center schoolhouse. The bear was reported to have weighed one-thousand pounds. Such an occurrence was extremely rare by this late date.

The population of the township in 1890 was 1,560 residents.

In the 1903 *Biographical Memoirs of Wells County, Indiana*, Rockcreek Township was said to be the most improved township in Wells County, if not in the whole state of Indiana. The township was noted for its many big red barns, which at the time indicated prosperity.

The Cover Bridge built in 1869, was named for L. A. Cover who donated land for the bridge. It was Wells County's last surviving covered bridge. It was burned and completely destroyed by vandals in 1966.

J. A. Brickley taught at the Rockcreek Township District #2 school.

Rockcreek School #8

Sugar Grove school is located south of Uniondale. It was built in 1898 and has been a private residence since the 1930s.

ROCKFORD/BARBERS MILL

Rockford lies in the southwest corner of the township, about seven miles west of Bluffton. The village was platted on September 21, 1849, by Solomon Johnson and Matthew Davis. Rockford became the trading center for the township as early as 1849.

The post office, known as Barber's Mill, was established August 4, 1852, by Postmaster Emerson Barber. Benjamin Brown was the first postmaster. The post office closed on February 15, 1905.

Early businesses included Morgan Ware, general store; C. C. Swaim, postmaster, hardware, and groceries; William Johnson and Sons, blacksmith; H. F. Lucabaugh, dry goods and groceries; Brown and Ware, tile factory; Braner Brothers, tile factory; Milton Davis, sawmill; and Doctors J. W. and C. H. English, physicians. The Redding and Coolman tile factory, started in 1886, was a mile and a half south of Rockford. An effort was once made to establish a saloon, but it very quickly went out of business. It should be noted, too, that stone was quarried out of Rockford for many years.

The Reverend Hallet Barber built a waterpower saw and gristmill on the banks of Rock Creek. One day in March 1877, an engine exploded, killing two men and wounding several others. The mill was never rebuilt.

The village also had a Red Man Lodge at one time. In 1914 the population was one hundred residents. There was no post office at that time, but three general stores were still in business. At one time John McBride ran one of the general stores, and also had a huckster wagon. Charles A. Bowman ran the Linhart & Bowman general store. Mark Swank owned the store in later years. It was noted for its ice cream and was a local gathering place where men played checkers. Soon however, the popularity of the automobile caused shopping patterns to change, and the general store disappeared from the scene.

The old one room schoolhouse was torn down in 1922 and replaced the next year with the new Rockcreek Township school. A grand total of 708 students graduated from the school. The last graduating class was in 1964. The school was torn down in 1980. The alumni erected this marker near the corner of 300 North and 300 West in honor of the old school.

In the 1930s croquet tournaments were played on courts south of the general store. Jim Wells was a barber for many years. In 1943, Rockford had a bad flood which affected every aspect of life.

TRACY/MADDUXVILLE/MARKLE

Markle is on the border between Huntington and Wells counties. Only a small section of the east side lies in Wells County.

Early settlers around Markle from Wells and Huntington counties were Isaac Sparks in 1834, John Sheets, a Mr. Adams and his son-in-law, John Schoolcraft, Jacob and Reason Souers, Jacob Shively, and Gideon Lantis. Several years later, William Wirt (1848) and Josiah Roush (1850) settled in the Markle area.

The first log-rolling took place on the farm of Moses Sparks. The first mill near Markle in Huntington County was owned by Albert Draper.

In 1832 a Mr. Tracy of New York state built a log cabin on what is now the corner of Morse and Clark streets. Mr. Tracy returned to New York to bring his family back to Tracy, but died before they could make the journey. When he didn't return, three legal advisors from Fort Wayne purchased forty acres of forest around Tracy and platted it into lots. They didn't like the name Tracy so they named the place Markle after one of their wives' families.

In 1836 Elias Murray laid out the town of Markle. Doctor Joseph Scott, a physician, built the first residence in 1849. Tracy established its first post office in May of 1849. It was renamed Markle in June of 1852. George F. Miller was the first postmaster. Edwin Haswell was the first merchant. Other early businesses were general stores, a blacksmith shop, a wagon maker, a shoe shop, carpenters, a tan yard, a flourmill, and a sawmill. The first school was built in 1852, and Thomas Logan was its first teacher. The first bridge to span the Wabash near Markle was built in 1860.

Barbers Mills Friends Church was organized in 1892. Founders were Reverend Cyrus Williams and Reverend Myra (Vickery) Webster.

With the completion of the railroad around 1878, Markle was booming. New merchants were moving into the fast-growing little village. John Leeper sold groceries and dry goods, W. P. Bender and J. H. Rarick operated general stores, J. E. Baker had a drugstore, John Shelby ran a hotel, Marion Quick and H. C. Dilley established a livery barn, J. E. Harvey was the town barber, and Valentine Cupp was the undertaker.

In 1889 the town of Markle was incorporated with a population of 584 residents. The first board of trustees included John Stults, W. H. Michael, and John Henry Rarick. At their first meeting they passed several town ordinances. In 1890 plank sidewalks were constructed in town. The first mail carrier was Samuel Brubaker, who made two trips a week from Huntington, Browns Corners, Markle, and back to Huntington.

Madduxville was surveyed by John E. Beil. Simon B. and Jane L. Maddux platted the twenty-eight original lots on December 14, 1881. Allen's First Addition was surveyed by William Runkle on October 14, 1891, and later that month was platted by Franklin P. Allen. Madduxville and both of Allen's Additions are in Wells County.

This marker in the Friends Cemetery east of Rockford, marks the original site of the Barbers Mills Friends Church.

In 1893 the Cline Addition (once part of the Wildcat Reserve) was added to the town. On February 14, 1896, Madduxville, Allen's First Addition, and Nedrow's Addition were added to the town. Allen's Second Addition was platted by Mr. Allen in October 1914

Markle has had two newspapers. *The Markle Journal* was founded in 1892 by W. W. Rogers. *The Markle Gazette* was published in 1913.

There were several early lodges and societies in Markle. The Order of the Free and Accepted Masons was established on May 27, 1873. An Odd Fellows Lodge was established on February 28, 1871. The Knights of Pythias was organized on June 6, 1896. Ruth Lodge #118, Daughters of Rebecca, was established in 1875. The Modern Woodman lodge was established on May 17, 1900. The Royal Neighbors was started in 1922. The Psi Iota Xi Sorority was formed in 1925.

The Farmers and Traders Bank was organized as a state bank on November 30, 1903, with James W. Sales, president; Hugh Dougherty, vice-president; and W. S. Smith, cashier.

The population of Markle in 1910 was 670 residents. Markle was one of the best shipping points on the early railroad between Huntington and Geneva.

According to the 1918 *Standard History of Adams and Wells Counties, Indiana*, Markle's only industry in Wells County was a packinghouse which sold eggs and poultry.

Although it was not in Wells County, the historic Markle Mill's destruction by fire in June of 1967 saddened many residents. The mill had been built in 1858 by Ansel Thomas, and had been operated by four generations of the Thomas family until 1964, when the U.S. Corps of Engineers purchased the mill. They had indicated that the irreplaceable building would be preserved as a historic landmark, but instead the corps destroyed it.

—L. Sawyer

St. Paul's Lutheran Church is located on County Road 300 North in Rock-creek Township. The first minister was Reverend Hugh Wells. He served from 1859 to 1864. The present church was built in 1880, replacing the older church.

William Smeltzer operated a threshing machine. Threshing rings were organized by neighboring farmers, working together to harvest their crops.

The Cover Bridge was completed in 1870, and was named after L. A. Cover who gave the land to build the bridge. The total cost of the bridge was $7,576.15. The bridge was 207 feet long and was destroyed by fire in 1966.

Rockcreek farmers help with building a barn in the early 1900s.

O. P. A. Form No. R-30!

Serial No. C 30 256 05

UNITED STATES OF AMERICA
OFFICE OF PRICE ADMINISTRATION
SUGAR PURCHASE CERTIFICATE

Not Valid Before *June 16,*
Date

DUPLICATE

THIS IS TO CERTIFY THAT:

Name: *Charles Bowman*   Address: *R-1*

City: *Bluffton*   County: *Wells*   State: *Ind*

is authorized to accept delivery of
Twenty eight (*28*) pounds of sugar
pursuant to Rationing Order No. 3 (Sugar Rationing Regulations) of, and at a price not to exceed the maximum price established by, the Office of Price Administration.

Local Rationing Board No. *96-1*

Date *June 16, 1942*

By *Max C Holloway*
Signature of issuing officer

Wells   *Ind*
County   State

Registrar.
Title

To Be Retained by Local Rationing Board

Charles Bowman ran the Linhart & Bowman general store in Rockford. His huckster wagon was a familiar sight to many Rockcreek township residents.

Back in the 1940s sugar was rationed in the grocery stores.

At the Linhart & Bowman general store,
this coupon might win you a prize.

Rockford had a bad flood in 1943.

Red Braden a native of Wells County, pitched high school baseball in Rockcreek township. He later played for the St. Louis Cardinals farm system. In 1930 he played in Danville, Illinois for the Triple I League. He soon gave up pitching and returned to Fort Wayne, where he managed the General Electric team for the YMCA Industrial League. After 1958, Braden never returned in any capacity to the game he loved.

Tom and Ella Carson lived on what their neighbors called the Indian Farm, near the southwest corner of 100 west and State Road 116. Tom was an Indian from Oklahoma and Ella had relatives living here in Wells County. At the long drive that goes up to the house, Tom built two brick pillars there that read Indiahoma— half Indiana and half Oklahoma. The Carsons lived on the farm from 1924–1944. Then they decided to move back to Oklahoma.

Morse Street in Markle, Indiana, in 1908. Notice the dirt streets.

The Thomas Mill was built in 1858.
Four generations of the Thomas
family helped run the mill. Fire
destroyed the building in 1967.

Although the Markle Swimming Pool is in Huntington County, many Wells County residents spend their summers enjoying all the activities.

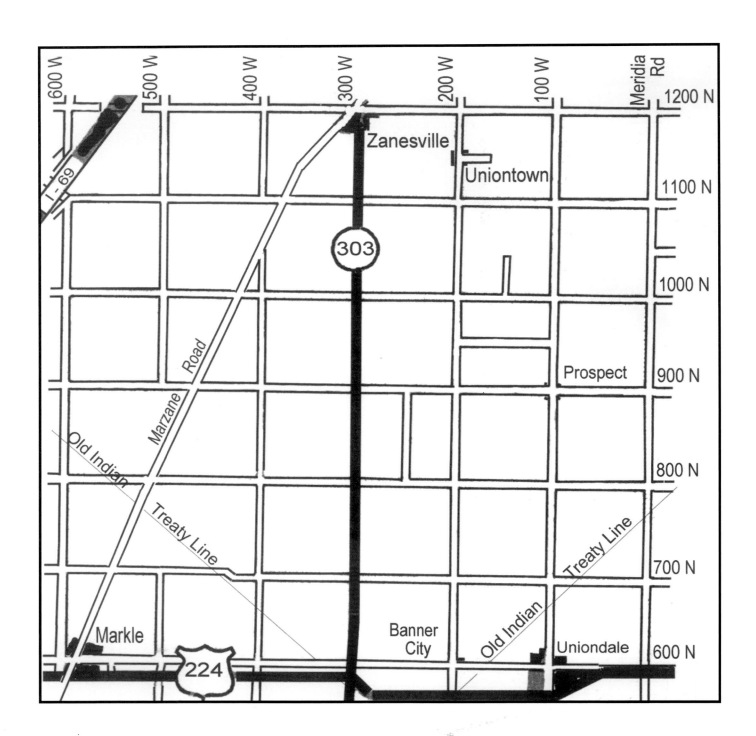

UNION TOWNSHIP

11

The first recorded visit of a white man to Indiana was that of the French fur trader and explorer, Rene Robert de LaSalle, during the 1670s. LaSalle reported that the Miami Indians were the most civilized of all Indian nations, were neat in dress, had good manners, and worshipped the sun and thunder. They were land travelers rather than canoe men.

In 1673, Pére Jacques Marquette, a Jesuit missionary to the Indians, in his search for the great river encountered the Miami near the Fox River region in Wisconsin. He noted that they were friendly, liberal, docile, and fond of instruction.

In 1718, the Miami men were described as being of medium height, well-built, with heads rather round than oblong. They were said to be agreeable rather than sedate or morose, swift on foot, and excessively fond of racing. They wore scarcely any covering and were tattooed all over the body. Therefore the English called them "Twightwees," an Indian word meaning naked. The women wore deerskins most of the time.

Me-Che-Kan-Nah-Quah, better known as Little Turtle, was the greatest of the Miami Indians. For many years he was the leading spirit among his own people and many others he came in contact with, either in council or on the battlefield. Wherever he was, he commanded undivided attention. He was a Miami, but not of full blood—he was one-half Miami and one-half Mohican. His father was a chief. Little Turtle was born in 1747, at the family village on Eel River, about twenty miles northwest of Fort Wayne.

Little Turtle was promoted to the honorable position of war chief of the Miami tribes at an early age. Through his variable career he maintained the integrity of his position with high distinction.

At the Treaty of Greenville, on August 3, 1795, the new government presented Little Turtle and the other chiefs with beautiful silver medals. Little Turtle remained the true and faithful friend of the American pioneers and the government. He was loved and respected by all who knew him.

Little Turtle died on July 14, 1812, after suffering from gout. He died in his lodge, near the home of his son-in-law, Captain William Wells.

On February 2, 1837, the General Assembly of Indiana, passed a bill creating Wells County. The county's namesake, Captain William H. Wells, was kidnapped by the Indians as a child and was adopted by Little Turtle. He was married to Sweet Breeze, a daughter of Little Turtle. Captain Wells served as a scout for the American army before he was killed at the Fort Dearborn Massacre during the War of 1812.

According to legend, a frequent visitor to the Zanesville area was Kil-so-quah, an Indian princess, who was born in 1810 near the Wabash River, a short distance west of Huntington. She was the granddaughter of Little Turtle. Her first husband was a Miami Indian (nicknamed John Owl). His death occurred not long after they were married. Her second husband was Anthony Revarre, whose Indian name was Shoop-in-a-wah (Thunder Storm). He was a trader of French and Indian descent. He died in 1846 and is buried near Roanoke. They had six children—a son, Anthony; a daughter, Mary; and four other children who died very young.

Kil-so-quah and her son Anthony Revere (Tony Loon). She lived among the English speaking people all her life, but could only speak a few words of English.

Carrying buckets of water was a chore. Weather permitting, clothes were washed outside near the water source. Heating the wash water over an outdoor fire kept the heat out of the cabin during the hot summer.

Kil-So-Quah died in 1915 and now sleeps on the western hills of the Little River, near Roanoke. Her burial place is only a few miles from Aboite Creek, where her grandfather Little Turtle gained his first victory over Labalme.

White Loon, the Miami chief in the Zanesville area, was Kil-so-quah's uncle. He claimed to have fought against General Anthony Wayne in the 1790s.

In 1800, William Henry Harrison went to Philadelphia to represent the Northwest Territory in Congress. He persuaded Congress to divide the territory, making the area now comprising the states of Indiana, Illinois, Michigan, Wisconsin, and part of Minnesota into the Indiana Territory. Harrison, the newly appointed governor of the territory, was also an Indian agent and was expected to protect the Indians from traders and frontiersmen. Harrison as governor was to persuade the Indians to surrender their land.

Many Indians opposed the selling of their hunting grounds and decided to oppose the Americans. In 1811, the Indians fought against Governor Harrison and were defeated at the Battle of Tippecanoe. Soon after this battle the Indians began to sell their land, and by 1846 had sold most of their holdings and moved to Kansas.

Union Township in 1847 was the last of the nine townships organized in Wells County. It is located in the northwest corner of the county. Until 1846 much of this land had been part of the Miami Indian Reservation, which extended from the southwestern corner of Allen County and included a portion of Wells County.

The land was covered with dense undergrowth and trees. The Indians hunted bears, deer, panthers, beavers, raccoons, foxes, otters, and wild hogs during the winter season.

Among the first settlers in the township were William Rosseau, James Edmundson, Joseph Rich, Milton Davis, Jacob DeWitt, John Wandel, Joseph Davis, and E. Bagley. Other settlers who came soon after were A. Housel, John Felts, S. B. Caley, Simon Krewson, James Cartwright, Robert McBride, L. S. Walker, Michael Mason, Henry Chrismore, William Bell, and William Walker. Many of these families came from Ohio, Pennsylvania, New York, England, and Europe.

The first election in Union Township was held in November of 1847. Joseph Rich was elected justice of

Union Township Center School was located in the center of the township. The school was built around 1875 and would later become Union Center High School.

the peace. He lived two miles south of Zanesville. On the first Monday in April 1848, an election was held in the home of S. B. Caley. The following officers were chosen: Joseph Rich, John Wandle, and J. E. Swalley, trustees; S. B. Caley, clerk; L. S. Walker, treasurer; William Walker, S. B. Caley, and Milton Miller, supervisors; William Rosseau and Robert McBride, fence viewers; and James Bell and J. C. Zeuts, constables. James Walker, John Feltts, and J. E. Swalley were also trustees for the township school board.

Abraham Beaber was the first teacher at Old Zion School, which was the first school in the township. It was built in 1848. Other schools were Ormsby School, Center School, and College Corners. Occasionally in the evenings these schools would have a spelling match, if enough candles could be found. All such social activities at the schools were well-attended and served to bind the community together. Some games played at recess in the early 1900s were common ball, lap jack, sock-ball, rabbit, tag, and mumble-peg.

Many of the old social get-togethers have almost passed from memory: quilting parties, taffy pullings, maple sugar making, log rollings and barn raisings, and even contests to see whether you could eat your length in sausage.

The first church in the township was Prospect, a log church built in 1848. Other early churches were St. John's Evangelical Lutheran, organized in 1860; United Brethren, 1855; Church of God, 1849-50; Church of the Disciples, 1853; Eight-Mile District Brethren Church, 1853; and the German Baptist Church, 1875. Big revivals and camp meetings often furnished much excitement.

Uniontown Church of God was built in 1830. Beside the present church is the Uniontown cemetery and about one-fourth mile behind this cemetery is the Old Uniontown cemetery. The first person buried in the old cemetery was Amos Walker, son of William Walker. The church still has Sunday services each week.

The land for the Hoverstock Cemetery was donated to the community by William and Margaret Hoverstock in memory of William's parents, Jacob and Phoebe.

Knight's Department Store was one of Zanesville's oldest businesses.

Samuel B. Caley and his son, George F. Caley, had the first mail route in the township. They rode to Roanoke by horseback to get the mail, and then people came to their house to pick it up. In 1854 a township library was established. The books were kept at the homes of the township trustees and were highly prized by those who were permitted to read them.

In 1880 the main road through the township was the Indianapolis Road, which went from Zanesville to Markle. By 1887 the township population had reached 1,600. Towns located in Union Township were Uniontown, Zanesville, Banner City-Waikel, Uniondale, and Prospect.

BANNER CITY-WAIKEL

Banner City became a village in 1860. It was along the Chicago and Atlantic Railroad, a mile west of Uniondale on the dividing line between Union and Rockcreek townships. The owner of the *Bluffton Banner*, Mr. Roth, named the village after his newspaper. The first business was started by Levi Waikel. Mr. Waikel built the first home in Banner City and was the first postmaster.

Banner City was platted on May 11, 1882, by John Crum and Andrew Brickley. John E. Beil surveyed and laid out 300 lots in April 1882. The post office was also established in 1882. Mr. Brickley bought and moved a sawmill to Banner City and operated the Miller Brothers Handle and Bat Company.

J. H Crum, Uriah Rarer, and Henry Folk all lived near Banner City in 1886. Levi Waikel's father, William Waikel, owned the first threshing machine in Union Township. In 1879, he handled over 42,000 bushels of grain.

Ice pits were located one-fourth mile south of Banner City. There was an ice house on the banks of the gravel pits, which had been used to make roads. Ice was cut during the winter months, packed in sawdust, and stored for summer.

In 1886, Charles Taylor owned a cane mill near Banner City which made molasses. The mill was run by his son, John, and Adam Hey.

By 1937, when the *Bluffton News Banner* published its Centennial Edition, Banner City had become one of Wells County's vanished villages.

A street scene of Zanesville in the early 1900s.

UNIONTOWN

The village of Uniontown was named for the township of which it was a part. The village was platted by William Rousseau, William Walker, Joseph Rich, and Robert McBride on December 6, 1847, in Bluffton, Indiana. Other early settlers were Mason Powell, Foster Barnard, Joshua Knewson, Z. Strong, Jas Shepler, John W. Walker, and Joseph Ellsworth. Its location was on a bluff that ran along Eight-Mile Creek.

The village consisted of a one-room schoolhouse, a general store, a blacksmith shop, a sawmill, a post office, and an ashery, which provided lye to make soap and hominy. In 1860 the first church was built.

What used to be the main street of town is now County Road 200 West. On the north, running east and west, was Washington Street. Center Street was the main street of the village, with Polk to the south. Jefferson was a north-south street. Jackson Street went east and west of Main Street. All the lots were sixty by one-hundred and twenty feet. The outside corners were marked by trees. On the northeast corner was a beech tree, measuring ten inches in diameter; on the southeast corner was a mulberry tree, measuring ten inches in diameter; on the southwest corner was a white oak tree, measuring twenty-eight inches in diameter; and on the northwest corner was another white oak, measuring thirty inches in diameter. The village was measured off in chains and links: one-hundred links equaled four rods and sixty-six feet equaled one chain. It might be of interest to know that in the middle of Section Two, one can find the remains of perhaps the first original burial ground used by the community. A few tombstones are still visible, but the site is completely covered with growth and is almost forgotten.

Herchel Wickliffe and Dallas Crismore stand in front of the Martin Wickliffe's store in Zanesville in 1905.

The Zanesville Basketball team in 1913.

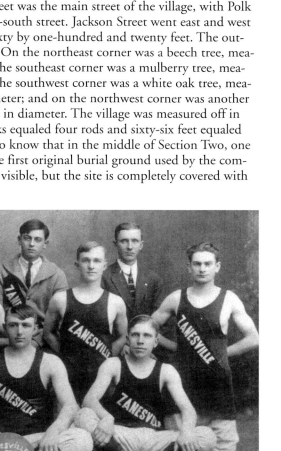

This sign greets people as they come and go around Uniondale.

Erie railroad station in Uniondale around 1913 after the installation of the double track.

Schoolhouse Number Two was built in 1851 by Stephan Cartright and was made of logs. Robert McBride donated the land for a cemetery and an orchard.

There are no present-day reminders of this small village, except for the Uniontown Church of God, which still has Sunday services, and the Uniontown Cemetery.

ZANESVILLE—EARLY HISTORY

Zanesville was founded on March 7, 1848, by James and Leonard Walker. Leonard Walker resided in Zanesville for six years before moving to another farm in Union Township. In 1874, he moved to Fort Wayne. He died on October 12, 1899, and is buried in Uniontown Cemetery. His widow, Malinda Davis, and ten children survived.

The town is near the northwest corner of Wells County, divided by Allen and Wells Counties, and lies along Davis Creek. The oldest portion of town, constituting about one-third, lies in Wells County. James Walker was the first merchant on the Wells County side. The Allen County part of Zanesville was founded on March 4, 1849. Henry Sink was the first merchant on the Allen County side. Allen County's Sink Addition was laid out by Henry Sink on May 16, 1857. Sink also operated a sawmill.

Knight's First Addition was platted June 16, 1877, by Conrad Knight. On April 17, 1878, he also platted Knight's Second Addition.

Zanesville most likely was named after Ebenezer Zane, who was authorized by Congress in 1796 to open a road through the Northwest Territory.

Early businesses included Knight Bell and Company and Michael and Hamilton, general merchants; F. P. Shepler, general merchandise and drugs; Reed and Taylor, carriage makers; Robert Clark, harness maker; George Biddle and Jonathan Michael, shoemakers; Cyrus Young and W. E. Angevine, blacksmiths; Kelsey brothers, meat market; Benjamin Mygrants, barber; and Doctors L. E. Murray, H. Z. Nobles, and G. F. Hesler.

Jonathan Michel was born in Germany in 1832. He was only twenty-two years old when he came west from Maryland seeking his fortune. Michel had heard of this new town of Zanesville while passing through Fort Wayne. He arrived in 1854 with five dollars in cash in his pocket. In 1855 he married Miss Sarah Kline and they had six children. In 1856 he purchased the tannery, which he operated for more than a quarter of a century. He also owned a boot and shoe factory. In 1861 he purchased the Zanesville House, which was celebrated for its neatness and the good food that greeted the weary traveler. Jonathan Michel died on April 10, 1913, and is buried in Hoverstock Cemetery, south of Zanesville.

The Hoverstock Cemetery was named in memory of Jacob and Phoebe Hoverstock, whose son William and his wife Margaret donated the land on which the cemetery stands.

MAJOR EVENTS

The first school was built in 1876. In 1880, the population of Zanesville was 228 residents. J. L. McBride was the principal at Zanesville High School in 1888. The first annual commencement was held at Zanesville High School on May 7, 1890. At one time Zanesville had a newspaper, the *Hoosier Advertiser and Printer,* published by J. W. Keplinger. In April of 1896, the Zanesville Four Mill was destroyed by fire.

Zanesville has had its own post office since 1854. In 1901 the Electric Interurban Railroad was opened, and the telephone came to Zanesville the following year. In 1903 the bank opened. By 1910 Zanesville's Volunteer Fire Department had been organized. Some local businesses through the years were Zanesville Creamery, Zanesville Lumber Company, Richardson's Grocery, Shepler Motor Sales, Roebuck and Stinson service stations, Gaskill Grocery, Lingerich Meats, Wilson's County Store, and Woods Meat Locker.

Clint Prough was born in the late 1880s. He lived with his family two miles south of Zanesville. Prough always had a big desire to play baseball, so he left his family and went on the road to play ball. In 1911, 1912, and 1913 he played ball in Birmingham, Alabama. In 1912 he pitched one game for the Cincinnati Reds under the manager Henry O'Day. He only played the one game, in which he pitched three innings, allowed seven hits, one base on balls and one strike out.

Clint Prough was six feet tall, weighed 185 pounds, and was said to be very handsome. He had the nickname "Wee Willie" because of his size. He played for the Coast League with Sacramento for six years and for Oakland for five years. He later pitched for the Southern League. Around 1926 he returned home to Indiana when his pitching arm went bad. Zanesville considers Prough one of our "Indiana Legends."

The town of Zanesville was incorporated on March 30, 1992. There is a town marshal and deputy to look out for the residents. The town has fire protection from the Southwest Allen County Fire Department.

Through the years Zanesville has been a thriving community with several businesses and much community spirit. Zanesville was 150 years old in March of 1998. Every Labor Day weekend the town celebrates Homespun Days.

UNIONDALE

Uniondale, three miles west of Kingsland, was surveyed and platted in 1882 by George Ditzler as a station on the Chicago and Erie Railroad. The village was first called Union. All land south of the railroad track is part of Rockcreek Township.

Hand car and track crew near Uniondale in 1913—Robert Scott, Forrest Harris, Charles Harris, Henry Burnside, Robert Bartholmew, Dewey Harris, Joe Harris, Clarence Keller, Kirk Harris, George Miller, Ross Strausbaugh, and Fred Bailey.

Lloyd Douglas also wrote the *Magnificent Obsession* and *Disputed Passages*. He spent several childhood years living in Uniondale.

J. M. Waid's General Store in Uniondale, Indiana around 1900.

Homer Harshman's sawmill in Uniondale in the early 1920s.

Mr. Ditzler sold his mill in Murray, leased two acres of land at the southwest corner of the Gardenour farm, and built a new mill there. For many years this was the largest sawmill in the county and furnished all the building material required by the railroad for some distance on either side of Uniondale. Mr. Ditzler's home was the first built in Uniondale. Charles, his son, was the first white child born in Uniondale.

George C. Ditzler and Henry W. Lipkey are recorded as the founders of Uniondale. Mr. Lipkey built the first store there. When the post office was established on January 21, 1886, he was also appointed postmaster and served as railroad agent. He later became president of the Bank of Uniondale. In 1883 he opened a store with a partner, William Newhard.

In 1882 the railroad was constructed through Uniondale. The first train on the Chicago and Atlantic Railroad went through town in July 1883. Charles Porter was agent operator at the depot for fifty-four years. George Black worked for the railroad many years as a pumper.

In 1891, J. D. Hite, a butcher, also opened a livery barn where he rented buggies, carriages, and teams of horses. Jim Waid ran a store from the early 1890s until 1930, selling everything from groceries and hardware to yard goods. William Meeks and Oscar Newhard also built bicycles. The same year the Knights of the Pythias Lodge was organized. In 1894 a bank opened in town, headed by William Meeks.

Uniondale was laid out in three different additions. The Union Station plat was recorded May 27, 1883, and was the area east of Main Street and south about one and one-third blocks. Baber Addition was recorded November 5, 1883, and was the west side of Main Street and south one and two-thirds block. Merchants Addition was north of Otto Street about one and one-third blocks and included both sides of Lincoln Street up to the railroad tracks. This addition was laid out by the Uniondale Improvement Association and Margaretta B. Strausbaugh on March 15, 1909.

Logan's Place, the local hotel, was nicknamed "The Palace." It has been reported that George Ditzler built it for his head sawyer and the workers for the railroad. Frank and Pearl Gardenour opened a hotel and restaurant called "The Beanery." You could buy a tin of beans for five cents and eat them cold with crackers.

Main Street in Uniondale in the early 1920s. Looking south notice the Erie Railroad tracks in the foreground.

Lloyd C. Douglas, the author of *The Robe* and *The Big Fisherman,* was born in Columbia City, Indiana, in 1877. His father, Reverend A. J. Douglas, a Lutheran minister, pastored the St. Mark's Lutheran Church in Uniondale from 1889 until 1892. Douglas' last book, *A Time to Remember,* contains memories of his parents, teachers, acquaintances and places, and especially his boyhood years spent in Uniondale.

The Uniondale racetrack was built in the 1900s and was used until around the time of World War I. The track went around Farrell Gardenour's barn and house. To the west of the Gardenour's house was the horse racing barn. Grover Brickley owned the property that the racetrack was on. People would come with their horses and try to train them, and then go wherever the races would be. Lon Brickley trained some of the horses. The races were held on Saturday afternoons all summer. There were also races at Poneto, Montpelier, and Warren. Hundreds of people came and parked around the track, letting their own horses stand where they were hitched. Little girls came out, all dressed up in their white shoes and stockings, to watch the races. There was a great big cottonwood tree on the west side of the track where they sold hamburgers and pop. The pop was kept in big tubs filled with cakes of ice. You could buy bottles of strawberry, orange, root beer, and lemon pop that came from Fred Kain's bottling works in Bluffton.

Around 1900 the telephone was brought to Uniondale. John Fisher operated the first telephone company in town. Electrical service was established between 1911 and 1912.

The CB & C Railroad first went through Uniondale around 1909. It ran from Portland to Huntington, although it was supposed to run from Chicago to Cincinnati. It lasted fourteen years and had a history full of problems. The Erie Railroad and the CB & C had agreed to share the tracks between Uniondale and Simpson. This made double tracking for both of them, so the Erie let the CB& C use their right of way. When the CB & C didn't live up to their agreement, the Erie workers threw their rails off the Erie property.

The CB & C train passed through Uniondale for the last time on September 24, 1917. Frank Brickley worked on the section crew. Adam Handwerk was an engineer who was scalded to death in a wreck near Bluffton. Ray Cupp was the ticket agent.

The Gilbert Block was built in 1915. Main Street was paved around 1919. Ival (Abe) Young built the first radio ever seen around Uniondale. It cost him twelve dollars. The Buckeye War Saving Society was organized in 1918.

The jitney bus ran from Huntington to Bluffton. It stopped in town twice a day and held fifteen to twenty people.

The Liberty Guards were organized in Uniondale during World War I. Stan Allen was the captain and had about fifty men under him. Their job was to save the town from attack, in the unlikely event that an enemy should attempt to besiege the village.

Schoonover's Woods was on the west end of town where children often played. Families had picnics there in the summer. It was reported to have many beautiful wild flowers and perhaps even some peonies, Indiana's state flower.

The Blue Goose was the name of Uniondale's Conservation Club. This group was active in the 1930s and 1940s. In addition to their conservation interest, they played poker. They were responsible for the ball diamond in town.

St. Mark's Lutheran Church was organized in 1883 with twenty-three members. This old church was moved so a new church could be built. The new St. Mark's was dedicated on Sunday, October 8, 1922.

Uniondale Methodist Episcopal Church was organized in 1885. The present church was completed in 1917.

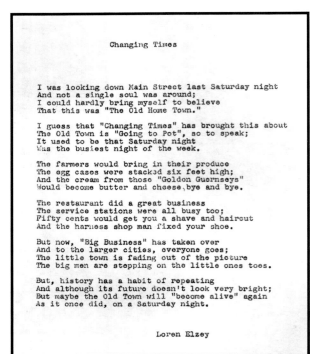

```
                    Changing Times


I was looking down Main Street last Saturday night
And not a single soul was around;
I could hardly bring myself to believe
That this was "The Old Home Town."

I guess that "Changing Times" has brought this about
The Old Town is "Going to Pot", so to speak;
It used to be that Saturday night
Was the busiest night of the week.

The farmers would bring in their produce
The egg cases were stacked six feet high;
And the cream from those "Golden Guernseys"
Would become butter and cheese, bye and bye.

The restaurant did a great business
The service stations were all busy too;
Fifty cents would get you a shave and haircut
And the harness shop man fixed your shoe.

But now, "Big Business" has taken over
And to the larger cities, everyone goes;
The little town is fading out of the picture
The big men are stepping on the little ones toes.

But, history has a habit of repeating
And although its future doesn't look very bright;
But maybe the Old Town will "become alive" again
As it once did, on a Saturday night.


                              Loren Elzey
```

Poem by Loren Elzey, a long time farmer in this township. He also ran a filling station in Uniondale. He served as county treasurer until his death in 1985.

Cupps Cabin sold meat, groceries, dry goods, drugs, and hardware.

The State Bank of Uniondale closed during the depression in 1930. In its place the Uniondale Exchange was founded. Loye Bayless worked there for many years. Local residents could cash checks, make deposits, pay telephone and electric bills, and apply for loans at the Exchange, but it too was closed after many years of valuable service to the community.

In the 1930s there were free outdoor movies for everyone on Monday nights and outdoor band concerts on Thursday nights, providing the weather was good. Everett "Bunny" Hare, a barber during the 1930s, was a friend to everyone. Cupp's Cabin, run by Ray Cupp, was one of the favorite places for men to visit. There were benches around inside for them to sit on. If a farmer made a trip to Uniondale during the day, part of his time was sure to have been spent there catching up on all the "news." The filling station was run from 1931 until 1957. They always sold Standard gasoline.

During the 1930s the game of croquet was enthusiastically played on the courts constructed where Jim Waid's store had been. The grass courts were carefully maintained. There were tournaments with different towns. Some mallets were expensive for that time, costing five or six dollars apiece. A fellow usually had his own special mallet. Some had a brass ring on the end. At one time Herb Brickley made mallets and balls out of hickory wood.

In 1939 the new road, U.S. 224, was built south of Uniondale. Through the years there have been many businesses in Uniondale. Restaurants, a tin shop, a lumberyard, a cement block factory, a grain elevator, grocery stores, a mush factory, hardware stores, barber shops, doctors' offices, a harness shop, a creamery, a print shop, a heading factory, a telephone exchange office, a race track, an antique shop, a tavern, and a vault factory, to name a few. Today Uniondale still has several fine places of business.

In 1982 the residents of Uniondale celebrated their 100th anniversary. Many people came to the little town to be part of this historic event and to meet old friends and share past memories.

PROSPECT

Many of the pioneers who settled near Prospect came from around Lordstown, Ohio, a small town near Youngstown in northeast Ohio. Prospect is located three miles north of Uniondale and one-fourth mile east.

The early settlers left families and friends behind. They came by wagons pulled by teams of oxen. The journey took almost three weeks, according to the information in a journal written by Hattie Wilson Redding. They settled in both Jefferson and Union townships.

By 1848 the township had three schools and three trustees serving the interests of the new settlers. Among the new arrivals were charter members of the Prospect Methodist Church. Having been associated with the Methodists in Ohio, it was natural for them to continue that relationship. Young families came to stake a claim and build a cabin, or young men came alone to establish a foothold in the wilderness and then return east to bring their brides to their new homes in Indiana.

These claims usually contained 160 acres. A few bushes drawn together served as a sleeping place. Then work began in earnest as cabins were built and the forest cleared so that the crops could be planted. There were not many roads, only trails to be followed through the forests.

In 1848 F. M. Palmer came from the Saint Mary's Mission in Fort Wayne to the home of Hezekiah Allen. Here the Methodist Episcopal Class was organized and called the Housel Class. The charter members of this church were the Allens, the William Cottons and their daughter Mary, the John Leppers, the Absolem Housels, the Websters, the Quackenbushes, and Mrs. Hannah Ady. These members held meetings in their homes, read their Bibles, and made their homes the centers of religious and social activities.

In 1853 someone suggested that the top of a local hill was a good prospect for the new church, so the question of name and location was settled. On December 22 of that year an acre of ground was purchased from Levi Osborn for eight dollars. The log church was

Present day Uniondale Post Office.

built on the northeast corner of this plot and the balance of the acre was used as a burying ground. The pews were sawed boards on a log framework. Sometimes these benches fell apart during services, which were said to be lengthy but spiritual. Many members came to church on foot, others came on horseback or in wagons, and a few probably drove oxen. Mud boats were not uncommon even in warm weather. These were sleds with very wide runners. Some of the trails were very low and muddy, even in the summer. Much of the forest was yet to be cleared and the drainage problem had still to be solved. Every charter member of the Prospect Church rests in the Prospect cemetery.

By 1862 the fast-growing congregation had outgrown their little log church. Funds were raised to build a new frame building on the newly purchased land across the road where the present brick church, built in 1912, now stands. The new church was completed and dedicated on September 7, 1862, with Reverend J. T. Nash as pastor. Revivals were the order of the day. Our generation today can only imagine the awakening power of the Holy Spirit as it was manifested in those meetings.

New names were added to the church rolls through the years. Among them were Sowle, Lipkey, Shady, Krewson, Osborn, Todd, Longshore, Scattergood, Newhard, Ashburn, Foughty, Wolfcale, Ormsby, Anthony, Sappington, and Wilson. These families left a priceless heritage of faith and service to this small community.

Each year Homecoming Day has been observed on the Sunday nearest the anniversary date of the organization of the church. The 150th anniversary was in October 1998.

Lenwell & Gilbert Bakery Ad.

PROSPECT SCHOOL

The Prospect School was a one-room log cabin school on the northwest corner of 900 North and 100 West. It was heated with a fireplace. The seats and desks were made of logs with tops and sides smoothed off flat.

One teacher taught all the subjects. The pupils were of all ages. The term was only four or five months long, and some children couldn't attend until the fall work was done. Sometimes they would have what was called a "subscription" school for a couple of months in the summer. The parents paid the teachers a set fee for teaching their children.

The children started school at five or six years of age. They learned to read, spell, and write. History and geography were learned from any books they could find. Some students learned to read using the Bible as a textbook. Pencils and paper were scarce. Lamps and lanterns were used to help light the school after dark. In the early schools a water bucket with a dipper sat on the bench in the corner.

—L. Sawyer

Old hardware store/lodge hall in Uniondale.

Historic Schwartz Building.

Horeb Cemetery was moved from the banks of the Wabash River to U.S. Highway 224 and State Road 3 in 1970.

This nature preserve is located on 800 North just west of Meridian Road.

Prospect Church—
Cornerstone ceremony.
The frame of the old
church was used in the
construction of the new
church.

The Prospect Cemetery
is across the road from
the Prospect Church.

BIBLIOGRAPHY

BOOKS AND ARTICLES

Allen, Harry. "Nottingham Township History." *Centennial Edition, Bluffton News-Banner*. Bluffton, IN, 1937.

Auditor. Wells County, IN. *Wells County Plat Books.*

Biographical and Historical Record of Adams and Wells Counties, Indiana. Chicago: Lewis Publishing Company, 1887.

Bowen, B. F. *Biographical Memoirs of Wells County, Indiana.*: Logansport, IN, B. F. Bowen, 1903.

City of Bluffton, Indiana. *Revised Ordinances of the City of Bluffton.* Bluffton, IN. City of Bluffton, IN, 1889.

Diffenbaugh, Robert, Joan Keefer, and George Bachnevsky. *Historical Pictures of Huntington County.* Huntington, IN: Huntington Alert, Inc., 1988.

Edwards, Melba, Rosemary Kumfer, and Velma Harden. *Zanesville, Indiana.* Ossian, IN: Ossian *Journal*, 1976.

Engle, Jeannine Shull and Ruth Garrison Jones. *The Little Church on Rock Creek 1887–1987.* Indiana, 1987.

Ericsson, Dwight and Ann Ericsson. *Forks of the Wabash—An Historical Survey.* 1991.

Griswold, B. J. *Pictorial History of Fort Wayne, Indiana.* Chicago: Robert O. Law Company, 1917.

Hardesty, H. H. *Historical Hand Atlas 1881.* Chicago: H. P. Hardesty, 1881.

Haymond, W. S., ed. *Illustrated History of Indiana.* Indianapolis: S. L. Morrow Company, 1879.

Huntington County Historical Society. *Huntington County, Indiana: Family History 1834-1993.* Paducah, KY: Turner Publishing Company, 1993.

Indiana Historical Society. *Indiana Magazine of History, March 1999.* Indianapolis, 1999.

Keefer, James H. *20th Century Souvenir Edition of the Ossian News.* Ossian, IN: Ossian *Weekly News*, 1900.

Leonard, Craig and Elizabeth Leonard. An *Architectural Atlas of Wells County, Indiana.* Bluffton, IN: Wells County Historical Society, 1986.

Ossian Historical Society. *Ossian-Jefferson Township: The Way We Were.* Ossian, Indiana: Ossian Lions' Club, 1992.

Rose, Dorothy and Joyce Buckner. *History of Wells County, Indiana, 1776-1976.* Bluffton, IN: Wells County Historical Society, 1976.

Scott, Beulah M. *Index of Combination Atlas of Huntington County, Indiana, 1879.*

Simmons, Richard and Francis H. Parker. *Railroads of Indiana.* Bloomington, IN: Indiana University Press, 1997.

Tyndall, John W. and O. E. Lesh. *Standard History of Adams and Wells Counties, Indiana.* Chicago: Lewis Publishing Company, 1918.

Wells County Historical Society. *Wells County, Indiana, Family History 1837–1992.* Paducah, KY: Turner Publishing Company, 1991.

NEWSPAPERS

Bluffton (Indiana) Banner. (Microfilm file, Wells County Public Library: Bluffton, Indiana.)

Bluffton (Indiana) Chronicle. (Microfilm file, Wells County Public Library: Bluffton, Indiana.)

Bluffton (Indiana) Evening News. (Microfilm file, Wells County Public Library: Bluffton, Indiana.)

Bluffton (Indiana) News-Banner. (Microfilm file, Wells County Public Library: Bluffton, Indiana.)

Indianapolis Star. July 10, 1994.

Ossian (Indiana) News. (Microfilm file, Wells County Public Library: Bluffton, Indiana.)

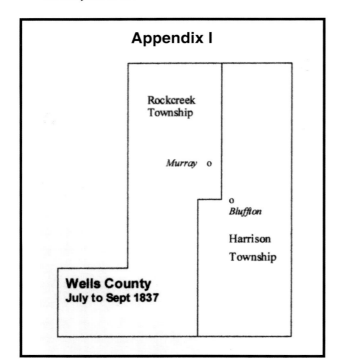

Appendix I

Rockcreek Township

Murray o

o
Bluffton

Harrison Township

Wells County
July to Sept 1837

Appendix II

Union 6-1-1841	Jefferson 5-3-1840
Rockcreek 7-22-1837 *Murray* o	Lancaster 3-1-1841 o
Liberty 6-8-1841	o *Bluffton* Harrison 7-22-1837

| Jackson 9-4-1837 | Chester 3-1-1841 | Nottingham 1-4-1841 |

Appendix III - Wells County Cemeteries

Chester	Lincoln	200 W - 1000 South at Keystone (Sec. 23)
	Miller	450 W - 900 South (West of Southern Wells School - Sec. 17)
	Snow	825 S - 475 West (NW Sec. 17)
Harrison	Apostolic	200 S - 800 East (Sec. 8)
	Bethel	450 E - 300 South (Sec. 23)
	Elm Grove	1 mile east of Bluffton on SR 124 E (Sec. 3)
	Grove	525 S - 100 East (Sec. 31)
	Linn	500 S - 600 East (Sec. 30)
	Six Mile	4793 SE - SR 116 East (Sec. 11)
	St. John (Vera Cruz)	250 S - 800 East (Sec. 17)
Jackson	Asbury Chapel	1100 S - SR 3 (Sec. 27)
	Batson	750 S - 750 West (on Willow Road - Sec. 11)
	Colbert (Old Indian)	625 South on Willow Road (center Sec. 4)
	Hosier	600 S - 1100 West (Sec. 5)
	Jones	700 S - SR 3 (Sec. 10)
	Miller	700 W - 800 South (center Sec. 13)
	Mrs. Tomlinson	950 South - 650 West (on Jeff Road - Sec. 24) (Right, 13 Graves)
Jefferson	Albright	675 E - 1100 North (Sec. 6)
	Bethlehem Lutheran	750 N - 650 East (Sec. 30)
	Elhanen	600 E - 1000 North (Sec. 18)
	Oak Lawn	South Edge Ossian, SR 1 (Sec. 15)
	Ossian	Young and Norwalt Streets, Ossian (Sec. 16)
	Prairie View (Tocsin)	700 N - 600 East (Sec. 25)
Lancaster	Fairview	1/2 mile east of Bluffton on SR 124 E (Sec. 34)
	Murray	150 E - 400 North (Sec. 8 & 17)
	Oakland (Craigville)	750 E - 300 North (Sec. 20)
	Old Bluffton	Hale Street, east of Oak Street, Bluffton (Sec. 33)
Liberty	McFarren	150 W - 500 South (center Sec. 26)
	Mossburg	125 South - 550 West (Sec. 7)
Nottingham	Bloxsom	150 E - 1100 South (center Sec. 32)
	Gearnand	650 S - 400 East (Sec. 3)
	Nottingham	1100 S - SR 1 S (Sec. 34)
	Old Salem (Salem, Kreps)	650 South - 700 East (center Sec. 6)
	Stahl	325 E - 700 South (1/2 mile west of SR 1 - Sec. 3)
Rockcreek	Emmanuel	500 W - 200 North (Sec. 30)
	Friends	100 N - 425 West at Rockford (Sec. 29)
	Horeb	275 W on US 224 W (west of Uniondale - Sec. 3)
	Methodist (Rockford Methodist, Spider Hill)	225 N - 500 West (Sec. 20)
	Old Cemetery	175 W - 300 N (Sec. 23)
	Redding	275 N - 500 West (Sec. 20)
	Sparks	325 N - 600 West (Sec. 18)
	St. Paul	150 W - 300 North (Sec. 14)
Union	Crismore	1/2 mile south of 1100 North and 1/2 mile west of Meridian Road (center Sec. 12)
	Hoverstock (Haverstock, Zanesville)	South edge Zanesville on 300 West (Sec. 3 & 4)
	Jones	450 W - 1100 North (Sec. 8)
	Old Uniontown (Crisamore)	150 W - 1150 North (center Sec. 2)
	Prospect	050 W - 900 North (Sec. 24)
	St. John	975 North - 200 West (Sec. 14)
	Uniontown	1150 North - 200 West (Sec. 2)

Total: 49 Cemeteries Identified
Published by: Wells County Historical Society — April 1999

Appendix IV
Wells County "One-Room" Schools

Union:

1. Bell (11)	6. Caley (17)
2.	7. Union Center (15)
3. Zanesville (4)	8. Prospect (14)
4. Splinter (9)	9. Buckeye (25)
5. College Corner (6)	10. Arbaugh (34)
6. Caley (17)	11. Needmore (31)

Rockcreek:

1. Sugar Grove (2)	6. Bender (13)
2. Haiflich (10)	7. Falk (26)
3. Shively (5)	8. Raber (28)
4. McAfee (20)	9. Rockford (29)
5. Center (16)	

Liberty:

1. Smoky Row (11)	6. Masterson (14)
2. Gaskill (10)	7. Wiecking (26)
3. Bly (8)	8. Popejoy (34)
4. Roberts (20)	9. South Liberty (Africa) (32)
5. Center (15)	

Chester

1. McAllister (2)	6. Gavin (23)
2. Slacum (Slocum) (9)	7. Maddox (26)
3. Noe (8)	8. Shields (28)
4. Red (17)	9. Five Points (31)
5. Center (22)	10. Keystone (23)

Jefferson:

1. Beck (6 R13E)	8. Jackson (17 R13E)
2. Castor (2)	9. Egypt (29 R13E)
3. Milikan (4)	10. Tocsin (36)
4. Bethel (7)	11. Beaty (26)
5. Glass (20)	12. Greenwood (33)
6. Ossian (16)	13. Frog Pond (20)
7. Bunn (23)	

Lancaster:

1. Little Vine (2 R13E)	7. Wasson (26)
2. Eagleville (4)	8. Toll Gate (27)
3. Donaldson (7)	9. Roush-Lamb (22)
4. Murray (17)	10. Little (31 R13E)
5. Center (16)	11. Craigville (19 R13E)
6. Bender (23)	

Harrison:

1. Gerber (8 R13E)	9. Travisville (19)
2. Shoemaker (5)	10. (32)
3. Schrock (11)	11. Grove (33)
4. Section (9)	12. Reiffsburg (34)
5. Poor Farm (11)	13. Myers Chapel (35)
6. Poplar Grove (12)	14. Beeler (31 R13E)
7. Smoky Row (23)	15. VeraCruz (17 R13E)
8. Hoover (21)	

Nottingham:

1. Kreps (7 R13E)	7. Coon (13)
2. Warner (1)	8. Domestic (18)
3. Stahl (3)	9. Harper (30)
4. Frog Pond (6)	10. Molehill (26)
5. Ternman (19)	11. Nottingham (27)
6. Petroleum (15)	12. Scott (32)

Jackson:

1. Batson (2)	7. McIntire (26)
2. Wiley (7)	8. Alexander (33)
3. Dillman (10)	9. Banter (30)
4. Eversole (8)	10. McNatt (15)
5. Batson Bridge (10)	11. Center
6. Jamison (23)	

Note - The school names listed were those commonly used. Some records show different names for the schools. Usually the names identified their location, or the name of the adjacent landowner.
Section locations from a 1905 Wells County Map by Cuno Kibele.

Appendix V
Contributors

George Warner, Beverly Stoner Patrick, Cathy Burnsed, Valerie Colburn, Robert Egly, Don Cochran, Dan McAfee, Jayne Decker Sullivan, Herman Myers, Finley Lane, George Risser, Don & Judy Shaffer, Wayne Frauhiger, Paul Bender, Alan Daugherty, Floyd & Marilyn Minnich, Dave Goodwin, Carl Goodwin, Robert Hoopingarner, Fred & Letitia Grandlienard, Craig Leonard, Ted Showalter, John & Esther Pease, Max Deihl, Robert Deihl, David Watters, Earl & Manette Watters, Joe Moore, Floyd Soper, Mary Smith, Maxine Thompson, Jane Jarrett, John Gardner, Robert Smith, Alan Smith, Ruth Oswalt, Donald Davis, Amos Gerber, Phyllis & Don Croy, Edna Wenger, Eileen Walter, Ed Rodenbeck, Mary Shoup, Joan & Bill Garrett, Gayle Miller, Marlyn Koons, Bill Campbell, Francis Bayless, Maxine Junk, Jim Foster, Tom & Mary Lou Woodward, Laura Sawyer, Marilyn Koons, Barbara Elliott, Robert & Eleanor Woods, Floyd & Sarah Caldwell, Joan Phillips Gordon, Harold Bowman, Ed & Reada McBride Espich, Melba Edwards, Ed & Avon Crismore, Anna Fullhart, Betty Oakes, Janice Williams, Letha Rupright, Jayde Brumbaugh, Gladys Cotton, Jack Liby, Barbara Girvin, Marilyn Kahn, Naomi Henly, Joyce Wenger Phillabaum, Ellen Cayot Decker, Mary Harris Cupp, David Park, Max Schwartz, Madeline Bowman Mosure, James Bowman, Gordon & Marcy Hart, Joe Smekens, Peggy Booth Bate.

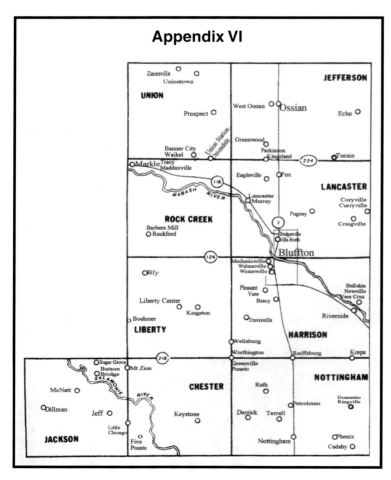

Appendix VI

Appendix VII
About the Authors

Barbara Elliott is the current president of the Wells County Historical Society, currently (1999) in her second year. Retired from many years service as director of the Wells County Public Library, she has had experience in academic and proprietary libraries, and is a trained chemist who previously edited a book on the production of uranium. Mrs. Elliott has gathered and compiled the information on Ossian and Lancaster, Harrison, and Liberty Townships. A native of Wells County, Barbara is a graduate of Indiana University.

Laura Sawyer, vice president and president-elect of the Wells County Historical Society, is an active volunteer in numerous civic and ecumenical activities, helping with the planning, organization, and execution of community projects. Mrs. Sawyer has been a Wells County resident since early childhood. She has been responsible for the preparation of material for Union, Jefferson, and Rockcreek Townships.

James Foster, Wells County Historian, served as president of the Wells County Historical Society for the years 1991-1995. A graduate of Indiana University, Foster is a retired educator in history and English, and is a long-time trustee of the Wells County Public Library. He is a native of Wells County. Foster wrote the Bluffton chapter of the book and edited the entire text.

Paul L. Bender, a charter member and incorporating director of the Wells County Historical Society when it was reorganized in 1952, served as its president from 1965 through 1968 and 1989 and 1990. Bender, also a Wells County native, is a graduate of Purdue University and a retired hospital executive. He has been active in many community and state organizations and projects, receiving the Sagamore of the Wabash award from Governor Robert Orr in 1987. The photos and maps used in the book were computer generated by Bender together with preparation of the information on Jackson, Nottingham, and Chester Townships.

INDEX